Let your misery be your ministry.

Let your misery be your ministry:

How to turn your tests into a testimony

Dr. E.M. Ernst

Copyright © 2016 by Dr. E. M. Ernst

Let Your Misery be Your Ministry: How to Turn Your Tests into a Testimony

Published by ZION Publishing House

Los Angeles & Washington, D. C.

www.zionpublishinghouse.com

ISBN 978-0-9983845-0-4

Cover by *Rightly Designed*

All rights reserved Josiah Generation Arts & Media Publishing – Against the Flow Ministries, T.V & Radio Show. © No part of this work may be reproduced in printed or electronic form unless permission is given. Contact us at www.atfm.org or info@atfm.org Riverside, CA

United States of America

Bible quotations, unless otherwise indicated, are taken from the *New King James Version* (NKJV). Copyright © by Thomas Nelson, 1982. Used by permission. All rights reserved.

Another version used is: *New International Version*, (NIV). Copyright © by Zondervan Publishing House, 1984. Used by permission. All rights reserved.

Printed in the United States of America

Dedication

This book is dedicated to the great "I Am". It is because of the love of Yeshua, Messiah that I'm able to write this book and share my experiences of how Yeshua healed me according to Psalm 23. He restores my soul.

This book is also dedicated to "the forgotten child" who made it to adulthood having come out of an abused house and family situation. I cannot use the word "home" because home implies a place of safety and comfort which I know many children do not have these days. For every abused child who grew up and got married, raised a family, and managed not to pass on the abuse to their children, I salute you.

I do know this book would not be possible and healing would not be facilitated if it were not for the help of God and His Son Jesus Christ, Who heals the brokenhearted, binds up their wounds, and sets the captives free. He whom the Son sets free is free indeed!

As I was going through my journey toward inner healing, the Lord told me I would make happen for others what He has done for me. God also told me through my healing process, I would have the authority and compassion to help set others free.

The intention of this memoir is to share things which have happened in my life because I know there are a lot more kids (and adults) who have suffered at the hands of people who were supposed to love them and protect them. They were neglected, used as punching bags, and forgotten.

I do know abuse is often a tradition passed down from generation to generation, but the cycle of abuse can be stopped by the blood and power of Jesus Christ. This book, however, is not solely about abuse. It is also about forgiveness, covenant, and confrontation.

The events are real, but the names have been changed to protect the **guilty**. I pray as you read this book you will gain a sense of reality for what is happening in our world today that very few talk about. There is a tendency to blame the victim, but can we really blame someone for an offense when the only thing that happened was that they were born?
I hope by the time you're done reading this book, God will have shown you a story that you can relate to in your own life and help someone else be set free.

Acknowledgments

I would like to acknowledge many of the kids in our youth group, family, friends, and pastors who encouraged me throughout the years to share my experiences that would help others meet the Savior, be healed, and set free.

Special thanks to my close friend, Anthony La Guardia who offered encouragement and wrote the music for my song, **"I am With Thee."** It is through this song I have found comfort and am reminded that God never leaves me nor forsakes me. I believe this song will lead many people to Jesus, and the **"Josiah Generation"** will begin.

I have much love and gratitude to James & Duretta Warren for their encouragement and assistance with this project. I truly believe our paths crossed for such a time as this.

I would also like to thank my husband, Tony, and my son, Anthony for their encouragement and support. This has been a lengthy project, and although I have been apprehensive at times to share my life, I know God will use this book to help many people be delivered from years of bondage and be restored and reconciled to God, by the blood of Jesus.

We have ministered to thousands of kids over the years, and I know God brought us together for a reason. It is my desire that all of my kids who read this book will remember something that the Holy Spirit brings to their remembrance and share with others how they were healed and that Jesus can also set them free.

CONTENTS

DEDICATION V

ACKNOWLEDGMENTS VII

CONTENTS IX

INTRODUCTION XI

CHAPTER 1 1

Don't be Alarmed. God Knows What He's Doing

CHAPTER 2 7

Getting Acquainted With Jesus Christ and the not so Christ-like Christian Church

CHAPTER 3 19

Back to the Beginning

CHAPTER 4 29

"My Grandfather—the Alcoholic"

CHAPTER 5 39

Always on the Move

CHAPTER 6 51
Baby Adam

CHAPTER 7 53
Finding and Forgiving My Father

CHAPTER 8 63
Government Housing and Life on Welfare

CHAPTER 9 73
Moving to California

CHAPTER 10 79
My Mother's Final Years

CHAPTER 11 85
How Stress and Trauma Enter

CHAPTER 12 91
Ten Steps to be Set Free

CHAPTER 13 101
Living Victoriously

ABOUT THE AUTHOR 111

Introduction

I decided to write this book in response to many years of being in ministry and helping people who have been through trauma, abuse, and severe loss.

Normally, I am a very private person and have shared my testimony only a few times. Some memories were just too painful to relive. God has delivered me in many areas. I believe He directed me to write this book because there is a **fatherless generation**, and God, Abba, Jesus wants to be our Father! I put off writing this book for many years, but I believe more than ever that now is the time!

I'm not looking for sympathy; what I'm trying to do is to point to the light! John 9:5 says, *"While I am in the world, I am the light of the world."*

If you have been in darkness, Jesus is the only light I know. When I think about Jesus and how much He loves me, I want you to know how much He loves you too-so much that He died for you.

If you've done everything you know to do and have done what the "world" says about how to get healed, just try one more thing if you're at the end of your rope. I'd like to introduce you to Jesus!

Jesus specializes in hope, love, and giving His people a new identity in Christ. If you didn't have a daddy or a mom who loved you, Jesus will adopt you into His family, and you can have His name.

I heard the LORD say, *"That which you have been through gives you the authority to minister to others."*

As I attempt to write my life's experiences, it is my intention and sole purpose, as I reluctantly put thoughts to paper, to minister to those who have been wounded and rejected; physically, verbally, mentally abused and neglected by their family, friends, and even the church.

This I know. Abba, (God our loving Father) never rejects us! It is by the power of His sacrifice, shed blood, death, burial, and resurrection of Jesus Christ that I'm even able to talk about these things.

It is my prayer that when you're finished reading this, I have not only pointed you to the Savior, but perhaps you have been able to relate to something I have been through and how Jesus helped me get through life.

Although there has been healing in many areas—some of which has been a process of decades—I bear the scars in my body and according to Psalm 23 He, (Jesus) restores my soul. Your soul is your mind, your will, and your emotions. The Holy Spirit is the One who leads us to truth; truth about ourselves, truth about situations, and how we face those things to move on.

Some people will read this book and think it's just a collection of stories; but this is my life! You may not know how to process some of the things I'm going to talk about. You may not understand how I was able to move forward, and sometimes I do not understand myself other than it being God's grace and His mercy upon the wounded.

Healing comes from God's word, His Holy Spirit, and many gifted Bible teachers over the years who have decided to talk about their experiences and not hide behind platitudes and false humility, or walk around with a smile on their face pretending everything is "okay."

Just because we walked down to the altar and surrendered our life to Christ at some point in our lives, doesn't mean all our problems go away. In fact, I think that's the reason God makes us deal with our problems because He wants us to turn to Him for comfort and answers.

I am a realist, and some folks have gotten angry with me because I choose to get real—real about problems and finding the root of them, then going through the deliverance process, wherever that may lead.

I have been accused of being negative, but **sin and abuse are negative and ugly**. It has been my personal experience that people, who never deal with their trauma, including abusive experiences they've had, **stagnate in their walk with the Lord**. These are the folks who only want to seek out pastors, teachers, and ministers that tell them what they want to hear, and unfortunately, are not being told what it takes to be **"made whole."** Jesus wants us changed with a renewed mind and a born-again Spirit-man.

Some believers get tossed around from one toxic relationship to another, and they can never put their finger on why they gravitate toward abusers. I think all of us grew up in a dysfunctional family to some degree or another, but when we hide the abuse, we perpetuate it and pass it on to the next generation. This is where the sins of the fathers get passed on to the third and fourth generations, and nothing ever gets dealt with. **The blood of Jesus Christ can reverse the curse.**

If we never talk about the trauma, which we have experienced, and surrender it to the Lord Jesus Christ, the enemy will use it against us as a weapon. This weapon manifests itself in rejection, shame, guilt, condemnation, self-hatred, drug addiction, eating disorders, self-mutilation, depression, suicidal thoughts, and cutting.

The enemy wants us to keep our trauma and abuse hidden! He wants us to hide in the shadows and wants us to be weak. The enemy does not want us to walk in our God-given destiny. The enemy hides in the shadows.

James 1:16 says, "Don't be deceived, my dear brothers. Every good and perfect gift is from above, coming down from the Father of the heavenly lights, who does not change like shifting shadows." (NIV)

Once we bring the trauma and sins into the light, the SON of righteousness, who is Jesus the Messiah, brings life to our soul. God's truth is healing for our soul.

The Bible warns us about false teachers, itching ears, and those who only speak smooth things:

Romans 16:17, *"Now I urge you, brethren, note those who cause divisions and offenses, contrary to the doctrine which you learned, and avoid them. 18 For those who are such do not serve our Lord Jesus Christ, but their own belly, and by* **smooth words and flattering speech deceive the hearts** *of the simple."*

It is my belief that these are tactics of the enemy to keep many believers in an immature and ineffective state, with no power to change things. (victim mentality)
When we have the belief that we do not have any control over our circumstances, we blame our failures on everyone else

and make excuses when we do not succeed. Our abusers and manipulators want us to believe we deserve their mistreatment, and it's our fault for what they've done to us.

The victim is always looking for approval and fearing rejection from the abuser or the manipulator. This can manifest as "people pleasing."

<u>It's time for the church to grow up and stop being tossed around by every wind of doctrine! Sometimes, I think teachers and ministers only teach the gospel of salvation and not the gospel of the kingdom, lest the believers be set free, because they want to amass followers.</u>

Paul said we must follow our leaders as they follow Christ. If you're only being taught the gospel message, and you're never being taught discipleship or how to live or change your life, perhaps you need to find a new place of worship.

James 1:6, *"but let him ask in faith, with no doubting, for he who doubts is like a wave of the sea driven and tossed by the wind. 7 For let not that man suppose that he will receive anything from the Lord; 8 he is a double-minded man, unstable in all his ways."*

Jesus did not come into the world to give us "church"—believers are the church! He came to set the captives free!

Isaiah 49:8, *"This is what the LORD says: 'In the time of my favor I will answer you, and in the day of salvation I will help you; I will keep you and will make you to be a covenant for the people, to restore the land and to reassign its desolate inheritances, 9 to say to the captives, 'Come out,' and to those in darkness, 'Be free!'"* (NIV)

My intention is to be "real" in this book. Yes, I am born again, baptized, a blood-bought believer in the Lord Jesus Christ, and I have momentary lapses of walking in the flesh. In fact, most Christians have momentary lapses of walking in the flesh. Even pastors, ministers, and televangelists are not perfect. They are just people! If they tried to project they are perfect, they lie to themselves and are in self-deception. The bottom line is we can't hide our garbage from Jesus. He knows everything! **Just confess it! Ask for Jesus'** <u>**forgiveness, be done with it, and move on!**</u>

This book was written to show people, even as believers and ministers of the gospel that we have issues we need to deal with. Just because somebody walks down the aisle and raises their hand in a church service or crusade, doesn't mean all their problems go away! I don't know who told them that, but that's a lie!

God wants you to come to Him. He already knows everything that's wrong with you. He just wants you to admit it, recognize it, and stop being deceived by the enemy. There are things I've written in this book that I have only discussed with a few people—when it was necessary to minister to their pain for that time. Being transparent with my life story and putting it into a book was not easy. Like I said before, I struggled with the idea of sharing my life in a book for many years. But, I was obedient to the voice of the Lord and am now sharing these experiences with you.

Part of the reason I believe that to be true (sharing my experiences) is many years ago, when I first became a youth and children's pastor, I saw so many children on the bus ministry whose parents were drug addicts and alcoholics. Most weeks their parents didn't even get their kids dressed and feed them breakfast before church on Sunday morning.

I was told by the couple who ran the bus ministry that some parents were so drunk and high that THEY would have to go wash the kids and get them dressed for church. The Lord began to reveal to me there were countless youth who share a story similar to mine (which I'll delve into later). He told me one day I would minister to them out of my own pain, and then show them God can heal them, and set them FREE!

I know some people will not like what I write. I may even get criticized and made fun of. This is part of the rejection I have faced my entire life. However, if one person comes to know Christ through my life, and they receive forgiveness and deliverance, then this book was well worth it! I cannot focus on the "haters." I have to point people to the **"Healer."** My prayer is that you receive any healing you need as you read this book and allow God to restore you. Then, you in turn, use your misery for your own ministry.

Chapter 1

Don't be Alarmed. God Knows What He's Doing

I remember praying one night a few years after I first became a believer in Messiah. I was home alone while my husband was at work. I was attending a small, Pentecostal church, and people there were not very nice. In fact, sometimes I think they tried their hardest to chase me away from the church. However, they were not able to chase me away from Jesus. No matter what you've done, where you've been, or what type of rejection people try to push on you, **Jesus is NOT like those people who reject you!** Jesus says if you come to Him, He will in no way cast you out! John 6:37. *"All that the Father gives Me will come to Me, and the one who comes to Me, I will by no means cast out."*

    The first step you have to take for healing to begin from mistreatment in your life is to ask Jesus in your heart and allow Him to be your Lord and Savior. You must realize Jesus is who He says He is. Jesus is God, and He is the only One who understands everything about you!

    The Bible says in Psalm 139 that He formed you in your mother's womb before you were born. In the book of Jeremiah, God tells the prophet about his calling to be a prophet to the nations.

I know sometimes we are faced with our past traumatic experiences and because of the abuse, rejection, or neglect we encountered, we don't even really know who we are.

We take on the identity people have assigned to us because of something we've done rather than because of who we are. We need to separate our "who" from our "do." Once the healing process begins, we have to look at ourselves in a mirror and admit we were damaged, not perfect, and never going to be perfect. There's only One who is perfect, and His name is Jesus.

It has been my experience that the people who are extreme perfectionists are the ones who have suffered rejection and deal with insecurity and inferiority. They believe because people reject them or their parents have rejected them that this is how God is. Somehow people have it in their minds that God rejects them based on their performance. This is a distortion of who Abba (GOD the loving Father) is and is NOT in the gospel of salvation.

In God, Jesus paid our debt of sin and everything that we've done wrong. In return, we receive His righteousness. Because the Father sees Jesus' sacrifice as the ransom for our sin, we no longer have to walk in the identity and the persona of that **"damaged person."** I use the word "receive" because there are many people who do not think they are worthy of God's grace, love, forgiveness, or redemption. This is a huge lie of the enemy!

Sometimes, we hear curses and other negative words spoken over us. While we were in our mother's womb, there may have been negative words spoken over us, including curses, and even spells. Growing up you may have heard the statement, "You will never amount to anything", or "You are a huge disappointment." Maybe your parents or adoptive parents told you they "wished you were never born."

Jesus said he knows everything about us, and there isn't anything we've experienced He hasn't experienced, too. He knows what it was like to be accused of being illegitimate. Jesus knows what it was like to be rejected, despised, gossiped about, abused, beaten, and in the end, eventually nailed to a cross and murdered for the sins of humanity. Our sins! **We** put Jesus on the cross!

When some people think what they've done is "too big" that God could not ever possibly forgive them, and they tell people no one can possibly know what they've gone through—think again! Jesus forgives the murderer, liar, thief, cheater, adulterer, fornicator, the homosexual, and everybody else who admits they're sinners and need forgiveness.

The point is that it's time to move forward, but sometimes you have to go back and deal with your crap first! Sometimes, you're going to have to go back and ask people to forgive you for some of the mean, nasty, underhanded things you've done. You may have to be like Zacchaeus. See Luke, Chapter 19 and return stuff you've stolen. I've had to go back and deal with my own experiences.

How God heard and answered my cry

One particular experience was in 1996. My husband was working nights, and I was alone at home every night with my eight-year-old son. I remember lying in bed one night, and I heard the house cracking. I immediately felt fear come over me. Although I was a fairly new believer at the time, I knew it wasn't God causing me to be afraid because it says in the Bible that *"perfect love casts out fear, and <u>fear involves torment</u>."* 1 John 4:18. I immediately cried out to God, and this pain, agony, and brokenness rose up out of me. I started to have flashbacks from when I was a child. I guess it was the house cracking that triggered something. I remember saying:

"God, if you don't fix this, I don't know how, and I'm not going to get fixed unless You do it. I give You permission to show me who I am, to invade my space, and reveal to me who You created me to be because I know that You know everything anyway, and I can't hide anything from You. Please help me!"

The following Sunday I served in children's church, and as the parents began picking up their kids, I saw one woman walk up to another woman to ask a question. The next thing I knew, the second woman pointed in my direction. My first thought was, "Oh, now what!" "Are the parents ticked off at me?" Well, that wasn't the case at all. The lady, who inquired about me, walked over to me and handed me a poem she had written. I had never met her, but when I started to read the poem, I saw at the top it had my name on it **"Specially written for Liz Ernst."** The name of the poem was, **"I am With Thee."**

I remember being shocked that she spelled my name right. As I started to read this poem, tears started to well up in my eyes because I realized it was the answer to my prayer from the night when I cried out to God.

I was overwhelmed by the accurate response from my cry to God. We tell ourselves that God hears everybody's prayers, but this was something that was just for me. He knows my name! I thanked the lady and went home. It was quiet on the ride home. When we got to the house; my husband asked if everything was okay. I was stunned. This kind of thing had never happened to me before. I've reread that poem so many times, I lost count.

I knew in my heart God was going to heal me. I had no idea how or when, but I knew it would happen. Twenty plus years later, so much has changed because God is faithful to His word.

Every once in a while, I would pull the poem out to re-read it and remind God about the things that had happened and the things that had not, as if He didn't already know!

About ten years ago, I was re-reading the poem, and I heard the Lord say, *"This is a song."* I thought to myself, *"Well, I guess it is!" "God, You're funny because I don't play an instrument. I don't read music or write music, but nevertheless at Your word, I will keep praying about this."*

Through the course of events, God aligned me with many gifted Christian singers, songwriters, and musicians. Some of them, if I mention their names you would know them; some of them you will know one day. Nevertheless, I gave my poem to five different people, none of whom wrote music to my song.

Suddenly, in 2014, I met someone who I became good friends with. He played the guitar and was a songwriter. He recommitted his life to Christ, and our friendship became kinship. I drove home from work one night, and the Lord told me, *"When your song is completed, this will start the next season in your life."* I asked the Lord, *"Yeah, Lord about that; it's been about ten years now. I gave the song to five people and nothing happened with it. What's the next step?"* I heard the Lord say to talk to my friend and give him a copy of the poem.

Well, my friend told me it's not very easy to write music to words—it's easier to write music first then the words. I asked him to pray about it and see what the Lord showed him. A few days later, he had me listen to a recording of the song, which he said the Holy Spirit gave him a download to in about ten minutes. When I first heard the song, I knew it was my song! This started the next season in my life.

Chapter 2

Getting Acquainted With Jesus Christ and the not so Christ-like Christian Church

In 1992, I met Jesus. It all started when we bought our house. I was commuting to Los Angeles and a lady I had worked for at two different jobs for seven years was killed in a car accident. She was not only my boss, but she was my friend. She was a Christian, and I believed in God at that time. I just didn't know His Son, Jesus.

We would get into deep philosophical discussions. We laughed, but we always got our work done. She trained me and showed me the "ropes" in a male-dominated tire industry. I worked my way up from clerk to department head in four years. I followed her to the next job, and when she was killed, I was devastated. I remember sitting in my living room crying into a dishtowel asking God, *"Why?"* She left behind a husband and three children all because some guy ran a red light, crashed into her car, and killed her.

I remember saying, *"God, I know you're there. I don't understand any of this."* I had a 1950's coffee-table Bible which I inherited from my mom. She received it when she attended Catholic school. I opened this Bible which was written in King James English. I couldn't understand a word of it, and when I opened it, I could smell smoke from the fires that we had at our house.

That brought back a whole flood of even more memories because the smell of the smoke triggered all kinds of stuff. I remember sitting in my recliner, crying for hours. I remember thinking I didn't cry this much when my mother died. Tears are cleansing for the soul.

Shortly after that, my son started attending a new day care and school, which meant my commute was different, leading to a new freeway exit. I started to pass a sign twice a day which read, "Bible study Wednesday nights 7 P.M." One night, I felt something tell me I needed to stop and attend the church service. I now know it was the Holy Spirit. When I walked in, I met an elderly gentleman, named Ozzie. He was so nice and friendly and reminded me of somebody's grandfather.

I started attending Bible study there regularly for six months on Wednesday nights. My husband was working the afternoon shift during the week, so he wasn't aware. My son was about three years old at the time, and I wanted him to attend Sunday school and start learning about Jesus. Since I was raised Catholic and Greek Orthodox, it wasn't a question of whether or not God existed; they just never told us about having a relationship with Jesus Christ. I even attended Catholic school. When we saw Jesus, He was always on the cross.

This church was different; they sang songs and were "Pentecostal." I didn't understand very much of what was going on, but I knew in my heart I was supposed to be there.

I got up one Sunday morning, kissed my husband good-bye and said, *"Anthony and I are going to church."* This went on for about six more months. I approached Tony, told him that Jesus was real, and that I knew Anthony and I were going to heaven. I asked him if he would like to go to church with us to meet Jesus. I told him I knew heaven was real, and if anything were to happen to us, I wanted him to be there with us one day. He decided to go, and we started to teach Sunday school together.

Wolves in sheep's clothing

We befriended the youth pastor at our new church whose name was "M." We got to know him and his fiancée, his sister's family, and his mom and dad. "M" was a good teacher of the Word. I asked him if I could sit in his class on Wednesday nights, and he agreed. Well, it wasn't okay with the associate pastor who approached me on a Wednesday night and proceeded to yell in my face and tell me that I needed to sit in the sanctuary with the other adults, and I was too old to be back there in youth group. When I tried to explain to him that "M" was teaching the Bible starting in Genesis, and I was going to be his helper, the associate pastor would have none of that.

His profession was being a prison guard—he was loud, controlling, verbally abusive, and combative. His wife, (we'll call her "R") was in charge of the children's ministry and Sunday school. She was just as bad, but she was sneaky about it. They did all kinds of nasty stuff to me to try to get me to quit the children's ministry. Whenever my Sunday school materials would come in the mail, "R" would never give them to me while I was at church. She would always call my house while at church and leave a message telling me to pick up my materials the following week—when I was just at church!

I remember one Wednesday night, she and her crazy mother double-teamed me in the nursery, closed both doors, locked me in, and started to yell and scream at me about something stupid. I just remember thinking, these people are nuts, and they should be glad I'm a Christian because I was in the world for a very long time! I would have had no problem getting in their face being nasty right back. Sometimes the "old man" gets a resurrection! They did all kinds of crazy stuff to us that I don't want to get into. I did learn this though—just because you're a "pastor" doesn't mean you can't be a big jerk and control freak! I learned how **not** to treat people. Years later, I found out they were involved in a church split and decided to quit one Sunday morning before church started. Really nice, huh?

Just because people go to Bible College where they become a "licensed minister," doesn't mean they don't have problems with pride, ego, narcissism, and try to control people. Witchcraft is a form of control!

I remember coming home one Sunday after experiencing a nasty "R" episode (nearly every week), throwing my Sunday school packet on the counter, yelling, *"I quit!"*

I heard the LORD say, *"Are you teaching for them or for me?"* I said, *"For You, Lord!"* He said, *"Then, what's the* problem?" "God, You see how they treat me and what they do to me. They are nasty people; please let me take them out!" I heard the Holy Spirit say clearly, *"I need you there to minister to those kids. I will take care of them."*

A year later, I dreamed I walked into the church, and the senior pastor was gone. I wasn't familiar with God speaking to people in dreams, so I told three people, one of whom was my husband. I thought the dream meant that the pastor would get sick or perhaps there would be a heart attack or an accident, and that's how he would be "gone."

Three weeks after the dream, the church was packed, and the pastor announced he was trading churches with another pastor. The three people I told looked at me with a surprised look on their faces. It is customary in the Pentecostal denomination, when a pastor leaves the church, if it's possible, they take their entire staff with them. This is supposed to eliminate loyalties to the old pastor and cut down on strife and dissension.

He also announced it was their last Sunday at that church, and the next Sunday the new pastor would be there. We were there for about a year after that and headed up the children's ministry with no assistance from other church members.

We never had a Sunday off, and one Sunday in June 1996, as I was getting ready for church, (we were getting ready to take a family vacation the following week), the Lord said, *"Today's the day."* I asked, *"The day for what?"* The Holy

Spirit said, *"I want you to resign from the children's ministry today."*

Part of the reason I believe God instructed us to leave the church was the pastors were not teaching the Word. They were using recycled sermons. I had notes in my Bible from the year earlier where the pastor was preaching almost the exact same message with the same scriptures on the exact same scripture, and it was almost the same message.

That day at church we told the pastors we needed to take a break. We never went back. Nobody ever called us to see if we were dead or alive. It felt like, while we were working in the ministry, we served a purpose for them. When we stopped serving in the ministry, we no longer served their purpose, and nobody cared. **There have been several occasions when people have told me they wanted my gifts, but they didn't want me.**

Years later, I asked the Lord what this was all about. This is what I heard the Holy Spirit say:

"Some pastors/leaders want you to serve them and prove to them how much you love Me. I already know how much you love Me, which is why you served under those people for so many years. You don't have to prove anything to Me. I don't love you because of what you can do for Me; I love you because you're My daughter. You don't have to earn My love. You already have My love."

So, we changed churches and started attending a systematic Bible teaching church, which was great at first. However, the pastor talked about the Holy Spirit a lot, but he never invited the Holy Spirit to the services.

In 2004, God started to do some miraculous things at our new church. The youth group started to grow. I was having dreams and started to have supernatural experiences where I would put my hands on people and feel what they were feeling. When I went to the church leadership to share my experiences, the pastor mocked me and asked me if I thought I was a prophet? He told me he would never ordain me because I was a woman, and that he was the apostle and the prophet of that church. **I would later figure out that people mock what they don't understand!**

Insecure men usually do not minister alongside women because they believe women to be inferior. Secure men welcome strong women as co-laborers in the Kingdom. I can't really say I fully understood what was going on at that time, but it was very disappointing and discouraging that the leadership of the church wouldn't listen to me. I wasn't sure if it was because they were blinded by pride or because I was a woman, or both! All I know is I was having dreams which were coming true!

For ten years, I felt like I was living in a cave in my own home. My gifts were restricted because ultimately the church leadership didn't want a woman serving in ministry. It wasn't like they woke up one day and discovered I was a woman! I had been there for almost nine years and was the only female youth pastor they ever had.

There are so many stories of persecution at this particular church, but I will only share a few more. There was one occasion when the pastors told us we were holding the kids in the youth group against their will because of a broken door knob that apparently made it look like we were preventing parents from opening the door to pick up their kids, since the door would not open from the outside. This is the enemy's job—to distort things, lie, and make up stories to get you discouraged. People love lies and distorting the truth. People love scandal, even if it's not true.

I remember one Sunday I was sick and on medication, so I missed the first service. The youth ministry met during the second service. The requirement they had for leadership was that we had to attend one Sunday service. Even after I explained to the assistant pastor and the senior pastor that I was ill, they said we had to start "signing in" on Sunday mornings. However, we were the only people in ministry that had this requirement! Every Sunday it was some new rule for us only. They were trying to make our life so miserable and uncomfortable because they wanted us to quit. One of the associate pastors' nick-named me the **"Maverick"** because I questioned why new rules were made only for me. They commented and said that we should follow them "blindly."

Things got even more interesting when I felt that every time I turned around, I was under attack. There was a guy who used to live in the area twenty years before. He came back and started to attend our church. He did not like me nor the fact I was a woman youth pastor. At first, he tried to get on the good side of my pastor and started talking crap about me. This guy told the pastor I was only fit to teach women and children. I shouldn't be in charge of impressionable young men. We will call this person "D."

At first, "D" couldn't get an audience with the pastor, so he moved on to the assistant pastor. Then, "D" started attending our Friday night youth movie nights. This was evangelistic in nature, and the junior high and high school kids could invite their friends. We would show Christian movies, worship, eat snacks, present the gospel, and invite them to church the following Sunday.

One Friday night after the movie, I started to give the message, and the guy, "D", takes his Bible, throws it on the floor, then gets up and walks out. I finished the message, went and talked to my husband, and told him we were going to have problems with this dude.

My husband assured me it was a misunderstanding, and I should not take it too seriously. Well, the next Friday, "D" asks to talk to my husband in another room. In the meantime, "D" totally ignores me when I say, *"Hi"* to him; he acts like I'm not there. He proceeds to talk to my husband about how he should be giving the message that I'm only fit to teach women and children, and I have no business being a youth pastor. My husband didn't give "D" the response he was looking for.

"D" found an ally in the associate pastor, who later conspired to do everything in his power to get me removed from ministry. Guess who they put in charge after they kicked us out?

You guessed it, "D!" Well, "D" lasted six months. He took the kids on a retreat that we had planned and raised money for. The retreat turned out to be a total disaster. Some of the parents threatened to sue the church! One of the older boys who did not go on the retreat, but his cousins did, commented to the pastor, *"If Liz were there none of this would have happened!"* He was correct!

Another Sunday after service, I was walking around our youth room and asked the Lord, *"Why am I here?" "Why did you make it this way?" "Why are they trying to make my life hell?" "I live my life above reproach." "There isn't anything they can accuse me of, so why are they making stuff up?"*

I said, *"LORD, You told me to do this, and I'm going to keep doing this until they pry my butt out of here with a crow bar! God, this is not right; you need to be my vindicator!"* **A couple of weeks later, they kicked us out.**

The Lord revealed to me eighteen months prior that they would ask me to leave. So, when this all happened, I really wasn't surprised, but it was very painful and hurtful to me and to the kids in the youth group. Some of these kids we had taught since they were in second grade.

To make matters worse, after they told us to leave, they made us return to church on a Saturday night to pick up our belongings and turn in our keys. We were watched like criminals by one of the associate pastors. The following Sunday, the soundman called us and made a copy of the tape from the service. The senior pastor had announced to the congregation that Tony and I had quit. He said we came in the middle of the night, snuck our stuff out of the church, and some other vile things I won't repeat. It was all a lie! Later that night, we had about thirty people in our backyard wanting to know what the heck was going on!

After we were kicked out, it took me about a year to sort things through. I finally ended up feeling sorry for the pastors because they had no idea they were being so prideful and mistreating people. I asked the Lord what I was supposed to do. The Holy Spirit told me to forgive them and pity them because that's the reason their church wasn't growing! They recycled, used, and abused people so much, the church never really reached over one hundred and fifty people. They **"used"** people up rather than **"built"** people up.

The pastor is not our employer. He or she should love and have patience with new believers and offer prayer & counsel. Even if the pastor doesn't know how to help someone, he or she can seek out other ministries that can help. A new believer, in many ways, is a babe in Christ who needs to grow up. This takes time, months, or perhaps years. The leadership is supposed to offer hope in Christ.

Chapter 3
Back to the Beginning

My earliest recollections are as a young child growing up in a flat on Montclair Street in downtown Detroit. My grandparents, my mother, my aunt Kat, and I lived on the top level. My great-grandparents lived in the basement, and various family members lived on the first level.

It wasn't until I gave my life to Christ years later that some of my childhood memories started to resurface. It is my understanding when someone is traumatized, the mind blocks out certain things because they are just too painful to relive. This can be a defense mechanism. I believe Jesus started to give me snippets of things that happened in my life, so I could deal with them one traumatizing experience at a time. If the Holy Spirit had allowed my mind to be flooded with horrible memories, I don't know if I would've been able to take it.

Just when I thought I was delivered from one thing, another issue would pop up. Sometimes my mind felt like a flower garden. I would weed it and plant beautiful flowers, but then little "sucker" branches or weeds would pop up again.

This is how I believe our Christian walk is. We have to deal with the weeds in order to enjoy the flowers.

Although I have vague scattered memories of the house on Montclair, most of my memories started to come back from the house we lived in on Warwick Street, Rosedale Park, Detroit. We moved there in the early 1970's because my grandparents wanted to be closer to their business. They owned a bar, called the *Five Deuces*, at 22222 Fenkell Avenue, Detroit. (The bar was sold in the early 80's, burned to the ground, and is no longer there). My grandfather Nick was an alcoholic, which I cover more in Chapter 4. He actually owned several bars in his lifetime.

For my eighth birthday, my grandmother rented the banquet room at Farrell's Ice Cream Parlor. I was able to invite all of my friends from school, and it was a great day! My grandmother hired a photographer to remember the occasion. I didn't have many fun and memorable events in my childhood, but this was definitely one of them!

My mom and grandparents had to work the bar that evening, so after the party, a babysitter watched us at our house. When I say "we," it was me and my two cousins. They were siblings. My female cousin was a month younger than me, and my male cousin was two and a half years younger. He was about five at the time. Several months earlier, I remember going to Phoenix, Arizona with my grandmother and my mother to pick up my great-grandmother Stella, so she could come live with us. My great-grandmother who was in her eighties' only spoke Greek and was a little crazy. When my grandmother was preparing the front bedroom for her mother to come live with us, she purchased a brand-new bedroom set with a dresser and new mattress. The plastic was left on the box spring of the mattress when my great-grandmother came to live with us.

The evening of my birthday, my great-grandmother had votive candles and matches on top of the dresser. My male cousin scaled the dresser, retrieved the matches, and went under the bed to light them. The plastic from the box spring ignited. Fortunately for him, he was wearing fire-retardant pajamas, and the only injury he received was to his hand.

The baby sitter, who saw the flames shooting from the bedroom, called 911. I grabbed the dog, and we all went next door to wait for the fire department. From the neighbors', I called the bar, and my grandparents arrived just in time to see the fire truck putting the fire out with hoses blazing.

The next year we lived at the Mayflower Motel on 6 Mile and Telegraph in Detroit. It was a living hell! There were five of us living in a motel with no kitchen and one bathroom. My grandfather's drunkenness was even in closer proximity than it was at the house.

It was one long year before the house would be repaired for us to move back home. During this time, my mother was diagnosed with diabetes. Later, I would find out that she was a gestational diabetic when she was pregnant with me and was in a coma for several weeks. Unfortunately, my mother did not regulate her diet. She would consume sugar in massive amounts which affected her health considerably.

One particular incident, when my mother's blood sugar went out of control, it caused a reverberating affect in the whole household. Her blood sugar climbed past 400, and she was admitted to the Henry Ford Hospital. The normal blood sugar range is 80-120. If levels get out of control, a person can go into a coma.

This particular night, my grandmother was working the bar, while my grandfather was at the hotel room sleeping off one of his drunken stupors. I decided to watch the TV show, "The Jefferson's", which was a bad idea considering my grandfather had forbidden me to watch any shows with black people in the cast, as you'll learn in the next chapter. As a result, because he was drunk, he started throwing things at me, then proceeded to slap me across my face, nearly knocking me unconscious.

My grandfather Nick hit me so hard, I could barely see. In that moment, I wanted to get as far away from him as I could. So, I grabbed my dog, and I ran to the motel office. I told them I needed to call my mom right away. My mom discharged herself from the hospital, got a taxi, and came to the motel. After she arrived at the motel and asked me what had happened, she called the police and had my grandfather arrested for assault and battery. The judge ordered my grandfather to a psychiatric hospital in Northville, Michigan to get help for his alcoholism. Keep in mind, I was eight years old at the time.

I went to visit my grandfather after he had already been in the hospital for several weeks. Part of his therapy was to make crafts, so he made me a jewelry box and some ceramic figurines. This is what I believed to be his veiled attempt at an apology. Most of what my grandfather did while he was drunk, he would not remember. Sometimes, he would drink so much, he would sweat the alcohol through his skin.

It wasn't until my grandfather had a stroke, and I was responsible for taking care of both he and my grandmother, along with my mother, that he was able to ask for my forgiveness. At this point in my life, I hadn't forgiven my grandfather and wasn't aware that unforgiveness holds us back.

The second fire

After the nightmare of the Mayflower Motel, we were able to return to our house and resume as close to a normal life as we had before.

My grandmother had a bad habit of smoking Chesterfield King cigarettes, which were cigarettes with no filters. Unless the cigarette was totally extinguished, it continued to burn. As a result, my grandmother had set a few trash cans on fire at the bar because her cigarettes had not been properly extinguished.

One night my aunt Kat drove my grandmother to work the bar. The bar was about four or five miles away. (I'd like to remind you that I was still about nine years old.) They left me at home by myself again. Before my grandmother left the house, she decided she was going to empty the ashtray. Once again, her cigarette was not properly extinguished, and the trash can in the utility closet caught fire.

As I was in the living room watching television, I looked up and noticed there was a cloud of smoke above my head. I got up and walked into the kitchen to find out where the smoke was coming from and saw the utility closet engulfed in flames. It was truly a miracle that the cans of cleaning chemicals which were on the top shelf of the utility closet did not explode.

Remembering what had happened during the first fire, I grabbed the dog, called 911, and walked over to the neighbor's house, again! Once I was at the neighbor's house, I called the bar and talked to Aunt Kat about what happened.

Aunt Kat and my grandmother got home just as the fire department was extinguishing the fire. This time the firemen went through the back where the kitchen was and broke out all the windows in the kitchen, breakfast nook, and dining room area. There was water everywhere. I saw the look on my grandmother's face. She was in tears and said, *"Not again!"*

The next call my grandmother made was to our local priest because she was convinced there were demons in our house. I don't know if there were demons in our house or not, but she asked the priest to bring "holy water!"

The insurance company told my grandparents they would not pay the claim for the second fire, and we subsequently had to move. My grandparents had purchased the house on a "land contract," so the house reverted back to the original owner. I would find out years later from an old friend that a couple purchased the house after we moved. I was told that the husband murdered the wife in the house. I have not been able to find any evidence of that.

For a season after the fires, I lived with my aunt Star in St. Clair Shores. Since my cousin and I were only a month apart, we were in the same class. Someone thought it would be cute to dress us alike, and people asked if we were twins, although we looked nothing alike.

While I was there, Aunt Star would frequently get drunk with the neighbors and lock us out of the house. Her husband, "J" worked at General Motors on the night shift. Some days when he would come home from work, he did not like what Aunt Star prepared for him to eat. One night I saw him throw the plate up against the wall and then proceed to beat her.

Sometime later, my grandmother and Aunt Kat came to visit me. They asked me how I was doing, and I told them about the beating. My grandmother was furious and confronted Aunt Star and her husband, Uncle "J". After that, Aunt Star and Uncle "J" no longer wanted me living with them because I was telling their private business.

As an adult, I learned that Uncle "J" was physically and verbally abusive to my aunt. He was also extremely controlling. He refused to buy my aunt clothing or undergarments and said she didn't need them, since she wasn't going out in public. Although he would not buy his wife or children clothing, he drove a Corvette. I remember seeing it in the garage when I lived there.

Abusers do not want those they abuse to have anyone to turn to—friends or family. I know this, having been abused by my own mother for years. There were several occasions where my mother was very violent and would chase me up the stairs with straps, belts, coat hangers, and broomsticks to beat me with. Sometimes, it would be for no apparent reason.

My mom would just snap. I don't know if she had a mental illness or if it was a result of low blood sugar. I often wondered if my mother was behaving this way because of the abuse she had sustained at the hands of my grandfather when she was a child. I talk at length about this in Chapter 4.

Warwick Dream

Our family went through a lot in our home on Warwick Street. Much of the trauma I encountered as a young child is attached to that home. In 2006, the Lord gave me a dream about this house on Warwick, which would start a healing journey for me. The Lord revealed to me that I would have to physically return to the home before I could go forward in my walk with Him.

Here is my dream:

I'm at my old house in Detroit on Warwick Street. I walk up to the door with Anthony, my son, standing behind me. I knock on the door, and this little woman about three-feet-tall answers the door. She is wearing a black, granny dress with her hair pulled back in a bun. She looks like a little, old, Greek grandmother in her sixties', but she was also ancient.

As she opens the door, she says, "I've been waiting for you." Anthony and I look at each other and then step into the house at her invitation. As I observe how small she is, I perceive she is a representative of demonic strongholds that had been in my family for generations. The strongholds of control, manipulation, division, complacency, and a religious spirit.

I begin to walk through the house and take authority over every demonic stronghold, and eventually the old lady vanishes. I continued to walk through the house and ask the LORD for healing in my soul (my mind, will, emotions).

From that dream I realized although I vowed never to return to Michigan, it was time for me to go back. I had to go back in order to move forward. Once I decided to heed God's voice, He gave me a detailed plan on what I was to do, where I was to go, and where I was to visit.

When I visited one of my old neighborhoods, there was a lady I ran into, who recently moved back to Detroit from Anaheim, who was a Christian. I had an opportunity to share with her that God was doing a new thing in my life and prayed with her.

I went to the Warwick house, and the place where my grandparents' bar was, and sat in the rental car. The Lord showed me now that I was an adult and a believer, the things which I thought were holding me back—failure, abuse, and feeling robbed of my childhood, were very small compared with what Jesus died to give me—total FULLNESS! I had a feeling of desolation in this place, a famine for the WORD, and a stronghold of rebellion & Islam that had choked this area. I felt a huge breakthrough and the confidence to be able to move forward. I made the decision that I'm not going back!

Chapter 4

"My Grandfather—the Alcoholic"

This section of the book about my grandfather was really difficult to write. It wasn't until I became an adult and was in ministry as a youth pastor that I started to figure out why my family was so messed up.

Dealing with some of the kids in the youth group was challenging at times. However, I understood a lot of what they were going through- the abuse, neglect, fatherlessness, and having parents who were wounded and addicts. In order to help the kids though, the parents were always a part of that process. I felt the Holy Spirit lead me to take classes to become a biblical counselor, not only to help the young people in our youth group, but also to facilitate healing and mend fractured families.

It really wasn't that difficult for me to show mercy and compassion to the kids. It was the parents and the grandparents who I had issues with. This forced me to spend more time with God in His presence and to deal with my own issues. It was only after that the Holy Spirit revealed to me how important forgiveness is, and that if these kids were growing up in a dysfunctional family, they had hope because I had hope. However, this time I was there to point them to the Savior.

My grandfather was born in Greece and was the only son from a family of five. He had a twin brother who died and three sisters; Helen, Lucy, and my aunt Mary. My grandfather's alcoholism stemmed from the abuse he sustained from his father. My great-grandfather, I would later learn, was an abusive alcoholic to his family, as well. My great-grandfather used to beat my grandfather and hit him in the head with Coke bottles. I remember seeing the scars one time on my grandfather's head and asked him how he got them. He told me that when he didn't listen or his father would get drunk, he would be beaten physically. It was in that moment I realized my grandfather's childhood "sucked" just as bad as mine! This is the pattern.

My grandfather told me he never wanted to be like his father. However, my grandfather never dealt with his pain and abuse and ended up being an abuser and a drunk just like his father. My grandfather decided to self-medicate with alcohol. This led to a whole host of other issues that would later come up.

Grandpa Nick was also a chain smoker and would eventually die from a grapefruit-sized inoperable tumor which grew in his throat, causing him to suffocate. This was after he had a series of strokes which he walked away from. The doctors warned him to stop drinking because he had cirrhosis of the liver. Sometimes, he was so yellow and jaundiced, his eyeballs were yellow.

Growing up with my grandfather Nick was like growing up with Dr. Jekyll and Mr. Hyde. When he was sober, he was semi-normal—as normal as an alcoholic can be—but add alcohol, and you get an instant idiot!

My mother told me about a situation she encountered with my grandfather when she was a young girl. My grandparents were Greek, and my grandfather was born in Greece. My grandparents' marriage had been an "arranged" marriage. Since my grandfather did not approve of my mom dating anyone who was not Greek, he got angry with her one night and went to slap her on the face. He used to wear a big Masonic ring on his finger. The ring hit my mom in the bridge of her nose; consequently, my grandfather broke her nose and almost killed her that night. She went to the hospital and suffered for the rest of her life with sinus problems and pain. Later, I would learn that my grandfather tried to have my father killed. This is the main reason (I am told) my father fled Michigan.

My grandfather Nick abused many of the women in my family—his own wife, all three of his daughters, and me. My grandmother told me that in those days divorce was not an option, so she decided to stay with her abuser. **Abuse is a pattern that needs to be identified then acknowledged and dealt with. When the offenders and abusers will not acknowledge there is a problem, then you must cut off the toxic relationship!** Unfortunately, my grandmother did not have the mindset to do so.

Our family was ostracized by the rest of the family as a result of my grandfather's abuse and belligerent behavior, and this left my grandmother with no one to talk to. We were never invited to any family functions because my grandfather would get drunk and make a spectacle. On rare occasions, we were invited to somebody's funeral.

The Detroit riots in the 1960's were a pivotal moment in my grandfather's life. The story my grandmother told me was that they used to own another bar called the "Finnwell." One night during the riots, they were closing the bar, and two men attacked my grandparents. One of the men hit my grandfather in the head with a tire iron, by which he sustained brain damage. At the time, my grandfather always carried a pistol on him. This particular night he did not have his holster, so he carried his gun in his pocket.

Shortly after he was struck on the head, he heard my grandmother scream as one or both of these men attempted to rape her. My grandfather then stuck his hand in his pocket, found his gun, and started to fire. He ended up killing one of the assailants. My grandmother said she heard what sounded like a bullet whiz by her head. My grandfather's injuries were life-threatening, and he was in the hospital for many months. I recall going to visit him as a young child.

After the riots, my grandfather was released from the hospital, and his alcoholism got worse. I remember hearing of a few occasions that he drove home drunk from the bar. He drove a 1968 white Dodge Dart. On his way home one night, he crashed the car into somebody's front porch. Thank God no one was outside, and no one was hurt or killed. He ended up getting his license revoked, and the car was parked.

We had hoped this would slow my grandfather down, and he would spend less time at the bar, but that was wishful thinking! He started stealing money from the cash register and taking taxis home. The cab drivers loved him because he would roll the money up and put it in his sock, sometimes dropping wads of cash in the back seat of the taxicab. All the cab drivers loved Nick, but they didn't have to live with him!

I remember one night I was about five or six years old, and my grandfather had gotten up in the mid-afternoon, after sleeping off his drunkenness from the night before. My grandmother had already left to go to the bar and relieve the daytime bartender. My grandfather was the only one home with me at the time. He got up, took a shower, called a taxi, and told me he would be leaving. I was extremely scared because I had never been home by myself before. Today, we would call this child neglect or child endangerment, but back then it was just my life, and another time "trauma" tried to creep in.

I think my mom was still working at this time, and when she got home and found out my grandfather had left me by myself, she was furious! I'm not really quite sure what the end result was, but I never remember being left alone again until I was at least eight years old.

The stories about Grandfather Nick are endless. This one, in particular, still stands out to me. One night, I was awakened by loud noises, yelling, and screaming. My bedroom was upstairs, and I ran downstairs to see what was going on. I saw my grandfather in the living room lying in a "pool of blood". He and my grandmother had such a bad fight that she took their wedding picture from above the fireplace mantle and broke it over his head. I remember seeing glass and blood everywhere!

The next day I heard bits and pieces of what happened the night before at the bar. My grandfather had been in one of his drunken stupors, yet again, and decided to chase the customers out of the bar because he wanted to drink by himself. He was behind the bar, and my grandmother was trying to get him on the other side of the bar to sit down and stop scaring people. (Keep in mind my grandfather always carried a pistol on him.) I heard it was at this point, he got so angry and agitated, he pulled his pistol out of his pocket, cocked it, and pointed it at my grandmother's head.

    I don't know if anybody ever called the police or if anyone ever came to my grandmother's defense. I just know all "hell" broke loose when they got home. I also remember my grandfather always slept with his 38 revolver under his pillow.

    My grandfather's alcoholism got so bad that he was drinking all of the profits from the bar. He started hiding wine and beer bottles in the men's bathroom toilet tank at the bar. He thought my grandmother wouldn't go in the men's bathroom. Boy, was he wrong!

    When I was younger, I had to sweep and mop the floors, along with cleaning the bathrooms in the bar before it opened. My grandmother showed me all of his hiding places, and I was to report any findings.

    I remember one time I was about twelve or thirteen years old, and I was staying with my grandparents. My grandmother was very sick at this time. My grandfather went down to open the bar. He had gotten so drunk, he passed out behind the bar, fell, and cracked his head open. Fortunately, a customer found him, and he was taken to the hospital.

    My grandfather's drinking would get worse because of the attack at the bar years before during the riots. When the assailants were tried for the crimes against my grandparents, the judge decided to give the surviving man a slap on the wrist, stating that the assailants' families had suffered enough. This is typical liberal speak—more concerned about the criminal's family than the "hell" unleashed upon our family by their hateful actions. This was a case of injustice!

About thirty years later after I moved to California, I was watching the news, and this judge was still on the bench. Unbelievable! My grandfather was convinced the judge was racist and lenient upon the assailants because they were black, and my grandparents were white.

As a result of the leniency the judge gave to the perpetrators of this crime, raging prejudice erupted in my grandfather. I was no longer allowed to watch television shows with black actors, and none of my black friends were allowed over our house. My grandfather believed that he had been treated unfairly and not gotten justice for his case.

My grandfather suffered three strokes, and with each of them, he walked away fine. The fourth stroke, however, put him in a wheelchair, which is where he stayed until his death in 1987. I remember telling my grandmother, I think my grandfather's stroke may have been a blessing in disguise because she was finally able to get some rest.

My grandfather used to sit at home and feel sorry for himself. I'd see him sitting in his wheelchair with his hands on his forehead, asking why this happened to him. One time I came home from school, and I said to him, *"This happened to you old man because you are mean, nasty, and nobody ever got any rest or peace when you were walking around."*

As a result of the stroke, my grandfather had a speech impediment. One day we thought we heard him saying he wanted a "space-heater." Turns out he didn't want a space-heater, he wanted a "faith-healer." Aunt Kat and I were almost on the floor, rolling and laughing. It wasn't because we didn't think God could heal him. We just didn't know my grandfather ever believed in God!

There are some fun memories of times I spent with Grandfather Nick. He was a master manipulator, and he always tried to get people to do what he wanted. So, every morning before I left for school, I had to get him dressed and cook his breakfast. Because he had been a raging alcoholic, and alcohol is nothing but sugar, he craved French toast, dripping in syrup. He also had to have a box of Twinkies every other day.

On this particular day for whatever reason, he didn't want to get out of bed. I told him he'd have to wait until I got home from school. He then decided he did want to get out of bed, but he waited so long, I didn't have enough time to make breakfast.

After school, I came straight home. Our front door had a little window at the top, and if you stepped up on the little stoop, you could see in the house. I used to step onto the stoop to peer through the window because sometimes my grandfather would be wheeling himself from the kitchen to the living room, and I didn't want to hit his wheelchair with the door. So, I would make sure the coast was clear before I opened the door.

I could see the kitchen from the window. I saw that my grandfather had pulled himself up to the counter and was making coffee in our old, electric, percolator coffee pot. I watched him for a few minutes because he had told me he couldn't do anything on his own—that he needed to be taken care of.

As he was getting ready to sit back down in his wheelchair, I flung the front door open and yelled, *"Busted, old man!"* He abruptly set back down in his wheelchair and started laughing at me. I told him he had everybody fooled, thinking he couldn't do anything for himself, and I told him, *"You're just a snake!"*

The sins of the father are passed down to the third and fourth generation. It wasn't until after I started scanning old family photos, I noticed that my grandfather, his mother, and my great-grandparents on my grandmother's side, were all drunks.

In the pictures were beer bottles in the bowling alley, at family functions, and obviously, at my grandparents' bar. The strange thing is my grandmother never drank! I remember from a very young age being around drunken people, folks on drugs, bikers, and the occasional prostitute. I knew as far back as I could remember that this was not my portion!

God had something better for me. I never had any desire to drink, do drugs, or take up smoking. I think I was the only one in my family who did not smoke, drink, or do drugs. **Addictions are a curse, and when you accept Jesus Christ as your Lord and Savior, His blood breaks the curse!**

I have hoped that my grandfather, grandmother, and mother could possibly be in heaven. With all their abusive behavior and our crazy, dysfunctional family, I know that Jesus is never without a witness.

Toward the end of his life, while confined to a wheelchair and thoroughly trashing his life, my grandfather asked for my forgiveness for all the years of abuse I had sustained at his hand. He told me he was sorry, and he did not realize how much pain his alcoholism and abusive behavior had caused the family.

I want to encourage anyone who is reading this—there is always hope! You may not be the one who presents the gospel or prays with your family member to receive Christ. But remember this, God gives everyone an opportunity, the space and the time to repent.

Even if you think your family member is without hope, God can still get through to their "spirit man". You can pray and ask the Holy Spirit to send someone to minister to your family member. You may be the "someone" who ministers and shares the gospel with somebody else's family member. And, in the end, you will be an answer to their prayer.

Chapter 5

Always on the Move

As a result of the insurance company's refusal to pay the second claim, my family and I had to move again. My grandmother found a house on Thatcher Street in Detroit. This was a little farther away, and each time we moved, I had to switch schools. I hated having to change schools.

I don't remember how long we lived at the house on Thatcher, but after a few months, we had to move again. I'm not sure why. This time, my grandparents had a room built in the bar that they called the "office," and they decided to live there.

My mom and I rented a room from a family friend with five kids. This house was in Redford. At the time, I was in the fourth grade, and we lived with her for about a year. I enjoyed my time there. They had a swimming pool in the backyard, and I became good friends with her three youngest daughters. I learned stories about Jesus at the little Baptist church in the neighborhood where they used flannel boards, and I was able to attend Sunday school regularly.

Another place we lived was on Otis Street, which was nearly inhabitable. The other place was on McMillan. Both places were extremely short stints before moving to New

Haven, Michigan with a woman named Shelly who was a friend of Aunt Star's.

When we moved to New Haven, I bonded with a teacher named Mrs. Lemon. It seems that no matter what school I attended, I excelled. There was always a teacher who took a liking to me. I invited Mrs. Lemon to one of my birthday parties, and even though she couldn't attend, she gave me a gift. I was so touched; it was two brooches which were little golden horses. Even though I did not wear them, I treasured that gift until they were stolen in 2008, when my house was burglarized.

Aunt Star and her friend Shelly had a falling out over the summer, which meant we could no longer live with Shelly. This happened to be the summer I had a serious fall which required me to get thirty-six stitches in my knee. With no place to go, we ended up at my great-aunt Faye's house (my grandmother's sister). We stayed there for a couple of nights. Then one of her sons came over, and there was an altercation between him and Aunt Star. Her son felt that Aunt Star and my mom were using his mother and playing on her sympathies because of us kids.

Now forced to leave Aunt Faye's, we went to another lady's house who happened to be a friend of my grandmother's when they were neighbors in Detroit. She was a retired nurse who was born in Canada. Her name was Mrs. Pringle. She was hilarious! She had short, red hair and lived on a farm in Utica, Michigan. She had grape vines in the back yard and plastic on her furniture. We stayed with Mrs. Pringle for several weeks while we waited for new, low-income apartments, considered government housing, to be built in Mt. Clemens, Michigan.

One day my mom told me the apartments were ready, and it was time to move from Mrs. Pringle's house. I recall getting to the apartment building and waiting in the car for a long time—several hours. Finally, my mom and Aunt Star said our apartments were not ready, which meant we had no place to go.

We ended up sleeping in the car for a few nights in a parking lot and had to wash up, brush our teeth, and use the restroom at a local Shell gas station. Being homeless was miserable, even if it was for a short time.

When the apartments finally became available on Lotus Street, we moved into apartment 101. My cousins lived next door in apartment 102. Although Aunt Star had furniture in 102, we had nothing. We slept on the floor and relied on the kindness of strangers, trash picking, and yard sales to furnish our apartment. Eventually, my grandmother would give us some of her old furniture, so we at least had beds to sleep on.

Surviving the Detroit Public School system

I enrolled in Christian Clemens Public School, along with my two cousins. Every school year I was on the honor roll except for my year at Christian Clemens. I had the worst teacher on the face of the planet named Mrs. "M." Mrs. "M" had a huge attitude problem. She was nasty toward me and other kids in the class. Later, she would chastise me for being white, and she was black. Prejudice is a two-way street.

I remember I had a friend named Lee Ann who I sat next to in class. My friend, Lee Ann, was not known for good hygiene practices. She often had body odor and bad breath. Plus, she rarely combed her hair or had clean clothes on. I just figured her parents were neglecting her, and I felt sorry for her. I think I was her only friend.

One day Mrs. "M" brought a metal washtub, towels and lye soap to the classroom. In our classroom, we had a coat room and our own private bathroom. Mrs. "M" stood in front of the class and said she was going to take people into the bathroom if they came into her classroom "stinkin'" anymore. She threatened to physically undress us and wash us with lye soap right there in the classroom. Mrs. "M" also said some of us needed to learn how to use deodorant.

She walked by a row of kids and assumed since I was sitting next to Lee Ann, the smell was coming from me as well. After the humiliation I suffered, I stayed home from school for several days. As a preteen girl, being told you smell and would be made an example of in the classroom by being bathed by your teacher in the public restroom in a wash basin with lye soap, this would traumatize anybody!

After a couple of days of me telling my mom I wasn't feeling well, she finally asked me, *"What the hell is going on?"* I told her what happened and what Mrs. "M" said. I showed my mom the note Mrs. "M" had given me. The note said something to the affect that I needed to practice better hygiene, and me stinking up the classroom was disruptive to the other students. When I tried to explain to Mrs. "M" later that it wasn't me but Lee Ann, she completely ignored me.

My mom was so ticked off, she discussed it with Aunt Star. Aunt Star then asked me to lift up my arm, stuck her nose right in my armpit, and said she could not smell body odor. The next day my mom contacted the principal of the school and requested a meeting. My mom showed him the note Mrs. "M" had sent home with me and relayed to him my experience in the classroom days prior.

I gave them a verbal statement, and the principal requested me to wait out in the lobby. The principal then requested a meeting with my mom, Aunt Star, and Mrs. "M." Mrs. "M" did not deny she had brought the wash basin, lye soap, and towels to the classroom. She pretty much admitted to everything I had said. Other students were interviewed and statements taken, but she was still allowed to teach in the classroom. She was asked to issue an apology, and later that year, I would be transferred to another classroom.

The next year, Mrs. "M" and her pal Mrs. "G" decided to teach sixth grade. Both teachers kept almost all their students from the prior year, with the exception of the "problem students," me being one of them. A new teacher started that year named Mr. Sampson. He turned out to be the best teacher I ever had. Mr. Sampson, Mrs. "M", and Mrs. "G" had math and science competitions between their classes. I helped tutor the other students in my class, and our class would win all the competitions, beating out the other classes!

Winning competitions between the classes was part of my vindication to Mrs. "M." Throughout the year, I also received awards in all subjects at the report card assembly. At year's end, I received the most scholastic awards and had the highest G.P.A. for the entire year. I also received perfect attendance and multiple honor roll awards that year and became Mr. Sampson's right-hand person in the classroom. I kept his attendance records, helped prepare lessons, graded papers, and excelled in every subject. In fact, that was the only year I had all male teachers for homeroom, music, art, and gym class.

My grandmother managed to save up some money to send her three grandkids to Catholic school the next year. For seventh and part of eighth grades, we attended St. Mary's in Mt. Clemens. It was an excellent education.

Toward the end of my eighth-grade year, my grandmother fell ill due to lung cancer. She was in the hospital, and I missed a lot of school because I had to take care of her and my grandfather. I was able to get my homework done and do independent study while commuting back and forth from Mt. Clemens to Detroit.

It was during this time, my grandparents decided they could not live in the bar "office" any longer. They decided to rent a house about a mile away, and we moved in with them. We were there for one year until the city of Detroit purchased the city block to build an athletic field for the local high school.

I tried to transfer to another Catholic school called, "Christ the King" in Detroit for the rest of the eighth grade. My grades were excellent, and they accepted me, but my grandparents could no longer afford the tuition. I was very disappointed.

I enrolled in Murphy Middle School instead. This was the year Detroit public schools decided to institute bussing. I was bussed from my school, which was a mile away, to Cervany Middle School. The round-trip bus ride added an hour to ninety minutes of travel time every day, which really stunk. I often tell people I should have shirts made up that say, **"I survived the Detroit Public School system!"** At least back then, they taught kids how to read!

    I managed to tough it out in middle school and enrolled in Redford High School the following year. Redford was across the street from the 16th precinct of the Detroit Police Department. In the 1980's, the school was like a battle zone. Drugs were just as prevalent then as they are now. I hated going to school every day—the textbooks were old, the teachers were boring, and the students were violent. After attending Catholic school, I felt public school was a waste of time.

    In the meantime, my grandmother had gotten progressively worse. My mom was sick, as well. Mom's diabetes was out-of-control, and she had a whole host of other medical problems. This particular summer her kidneys were shutting down, causing her to be in the hospital the entire summer.

    It was actually a rest for me from taking care of everyone. I had to cook and clean for my grandparents and make sure they'd take their medications.

    My grandmother was able to work until she had a stroke in her eye. She was a diabetic, as well, and refused to take her pills. One night at the bar when I was fifteen years old, my grandmother was having medical challenges. I had to step in and work the rest of her shift. No one ever questioned my age. I'd tell everyone I was thirty-five, for fifteen years! I always looked and acted more mature than I was and had way too much responsibility for someone my age.

The only time I was able to hang out with kids my age was when I'd go bowling a couple of times a week. Other than that, my life consisted of school, taking care of my family, and working at the bar. We had a weekday bartender for the day shift. My aunt Kat would work her regular job and then worked the bar with me until closing at 2 A.M. I would get up at 7 A.M. the next day to get ready for school and start all over again.

My grandmother's battle with lung cancer

We could not afford to pay anyone to work weekends or the night shift, so I worked for free. The bar also had a grill, which I ran and served food. Sometimes Aunt Star would "help," but later, we would find out she had a drug addiction and would steal liquor and money from my grandparents. We also found out she would have illegal card games in her basement, called "Blind Pigs," and furnished drinks to the players at my grandparents' expense.

As my grandmother's health deteriorated, we discovered she had lung cancer. The first response from the doctors was to do chemo and radiation. That summer, while my mom was in the hospital, Aunt Kat worked during the day, and it was my responsibility to get my grandmother to her chemo appointments. Although Aunt Star lived on the next block, she could not be bothered caring for her mother.

My mom had entrusted me with her vehicle, and Aunt Star was ticked off that my mom did not trust her with it.

That's because Aunt Star had a reputation of driving "deathtraps" and beating her cars into the ground. During this time, though, she didn't have transportation of her own, so she wanted my mom's car. Aunt Star was a liar, a thief, and a cheat. She was so hell-bent on getting custody of my mom's car, she made up a story and called my mom to tell her I had run somebody over with her car.

   I got back to our house one afternoon to find my mom sitting at our kitchen table. Mom had signed herself out of the hospital because Aunt Star told her the police were looking for me. Upon further investigation, my mom figured out my aunt had fabricated the entire story in hopes that my mom would give my aunt her car keys. We would later find out Aunt Star was a drug dealer and needed my mom's car to make her deliveries.

   Shortly after that, the doctors told us chemo might add five years to my grandmother's life, but she didn't last five months. Her immune system would be so compromised and her bones so brittle from osteoarthritis and osteoporosis, that she would be hospitalized. Then later, she would be released because of Medicare, which required her to stay home for some time before she could be readmitted.

   As my grandmother's primary caregiver for a period of time, I ended up wrenching my back because she was dead weight due to a broken hip. Toward the end of her life, my grandmother didn't even recognize me.

   In February of 1981, we were finally able to get my grandmother readmitted to the intensive care unit (ICU) at Henry Ford Hospital. The ICU was located in the basement at that time. Unfortunately, this was during the time of a major blizzard in the region which left us snowed-in the hospital for three days. The snow was coming down faster than it could be plowed away. We ended up sleeping on the floor and practically begging for blankets and food from the hospital. The five of us pretty much took over the waiting room in the ICU.

Once the snow finally subsided, we were able to drive home, but the snowplows were only plowing major streets, so the side streets were impossible to navigate. Our station wagon got stuck in the snow down the street, and we had to abandon the vehicle. We walked the rest of the way home. The snow was about three to four-feet deep, and ice was about four to five inches thick in our driveway. This experience ended up "topping" my list of the most horrible experiences of my life.

It would be a few days for the snow to melt before we'd get the car out of the street. We were able to visit my grandmother at the hospital one final time before we got the dreaded call that she had passed away early one morning.

We began funeral preparations for my grandmother, and none came forward to help with the expenses. Aunt Kat had to take out a loan, using her car as collateral to pay for my grandmother's funeral. We also did a benefit concert at the bar, so Aunt Kat could raise additional money to pay for her medical expenses.

My grandparents didn't have anything. Interestingly enough, all of my relatives came out of the woodwork, thinking my grandparents had money, which they did not.

Shortly after my grandmother passed away, Aunt Kat sold the liquor license, the fixtures, and the inventory. My grandparents did not own the building, so there was barely enough money to pay all the expenses. We decided to put my grandfather in a nursing home. When we moved to California, my grandfather passed away. When he died, my grandfather left me his eyeglasses, his wheelchair, his television, and his wedding band, which ended up being stolen in 2008, when my house was burglarized. Basically, I received nothing of significant value upon my grandparents' death, except chiropractic bills, five slipped discs, and multiple injuries trying to lift and care for them.

If I knew then what I know now, I would have never allowed my grandmother to go through chemotherapy. Chemo and radiation are standard operating procedure for the medical profession. If they can't cut it out or burn it out, they tell you there's no hope for you. Unfortunately, not much has changed in forty years, and I've found, as an adult, there are much better alternative therapies, such as www.truthaboutcancer.com.

Chapter 6
Baby Adam

This section, albeit short, is dedicated to all the children who have lost their lives to abuse and neglect at the hands of the people who were supposed to protect them—their parents.

When I was younger, I babysat regularly for a woman named Rochelle. She had a newborn baby and treated me very well. Rochelle referred me to babysit for another lady who lived in our apartment complex. She was a single mom with a newborn named Adam. This woman was Aunt Star's repeat customer, so I knew she was taking drugs.

Many times, she would call me to watch Adam, so she could go out with her boyfriend to get "high." On one occasion, she left Adam at home alone. I went over to her apartment for something and heard the baby crying. The door was unlocked, so I went in to see what was going on. After noticing there wasn't anybody there, I stayed with Adam until she returned.

I later told my mom what had happened, and she called Child Protective Services to report the neglect. I remember the lady was very angry with my mom and no longer called me to babysit Adam.

Several weeks later, I came home from school and noticed there was an ambulance in front of Adam's apartment. Adam died at only a few months old. I don't know if Adam died due to neglect or because he was ill. I just remember being devastated and asking God, *"Why?"* Every once in a while, I'll think about Adam and wonder if it was an act of mercy that the LORD would take him home. Was he spared a life of abuse and neglect at the hands of his mother?

I remember wanting to be older, so I could adopt Adam, in hopes that he would have had a better life. Charges were filed against his mother, although I am unsure of the outcome.

Chapter 7
Finding and Forgiving My Father

As far back as I can remember, my grandmother was always a little paranoid. She didn't even like me playing outside in the front yard because she feared my father would kidnap me. Little did she know, as I learned years later, my dad fled Michigan in fear of my grandfather.

I always heard rumors that my grandfather "knew people" in downtown Detroit that had Mafia affiliations. My grandmother would tell me stories from her childhood, living in Greek-town, about shootings and finding bodies in trunks, during the 1920's & 1930's. I'd often dismissed these as urban myths. My grandmother's brother, Uncle Tony, later confirmed these stories to be true.

Since I had never met my father, and I looked nothing like the Greek side of the family, I felt there was always a piece of my life that was missing. My mom used to keep a picture of my father in her wallet, but her wallet was stolen when she worked at Art Center Hospital in Detroit, as a phlebotomist in the 1970's.

When I was about eleven or twelve years old, I started investigating my father's side of the family, intentionally. I was told by my mother, my father was of Polish descent. I also had

DNA testing done years later and learned there was also some Jewish ancestry in both of my family lines.

One day I took the phone book out and started looking up my last name. I found one person in the phone book with my last name. I thought maybe my father had shortened his last name, so I started writing some other people, as well.

I returned home from school one afternoon to see my mother sitting at the kitchen table, weeping uncontrollably. I asked her, *"Why are you crying?" "What's wrong?"* She asked me, *"Do you want to go live with your father?"* I replied, *"No, I just want a picture."*

My mom told me earlier that day she received a phone call from someone I had mailed a letter to. It turned out to be a man who was married to one of my father's cousins. The man told my mom my father had moved out of Michigan, and the last they heard was that my father was living somewhere in Oklahoma.

I didn't really do anything with that information because I was young and didn't know what to do. However, when I was nineteen, I felt compelled to contact my father once again. I picked up the phone, called information, and asked how many area codes there were in Oklahoma. The operator told me there were two area codes in Oklahoma. I gave her my father's name, and she found a listing. She gave me his phone number, and I called him right away.

My father answered the phone, and I remember saying something like, *"I know we've never met, but I believe I'm your daughter. I don't want anything from you. I just want a picture."* He told me he had been expecting a call from me for quite some time. He said it was time for him to tell his family about me. I would later find out his current wife did know about me, but his three other children did not.

One really strange part of the conversation is my father asked me if I were getting married, and if I wanted him to give me away. I asked him if he was nuts, and why would I ask him to give me away when he was never part of my life? I told him he abandoned me and asked him, *"Why?"* We did not have a relationship. He acted like he didn't hear the question and just kept talking about something else.

He then proceeded to ask me about the back child-support he owed my mother and asked me if I was looking for back payment. I was really taken aback that all he was concerned with were financial matters, which were trivial to us building a relationship, and I frustratingly asked him if these were his only concerns. Though I do think he should have been ashamed of himself, given the fact I was nearly twenty years old and had to be on welfare because he wouldn't fulfill his responsibilities as a father.

I gave him our family address in Michigan, but the pictures never came before we decided to move to California. When we arrived in California, I contacted him again to ensure he had our new address. He sent me two pictures in an envelope that did not include a return address. I believe he tried to hide his address to prevent us from collecting child support or some other reason he feared, but little did he know I would get his mailing address from information. So, I mailed him pictures of myself.

My mother had always told me my dad denied I was his child. She figured it was because he didn't want to pay child support. My mom also told me my father was the only man she had ever been with, and it was ridiculous for him to say I was not his. It was eventually settled in a court-ordered paternity test, which revealed conclusively that I was his child.

After looking over the photos he mailed, I was blown away at the resemblance between the two of us. Although my parents were never married, I still had my dad's last name. Even though having children outside of wedlock is common these days, having illegitimate children was something that was looked down upon when I was born. There was a stigma and an embarrassment attached to being illegitimate. I don't think my grandfather ever knew my parents were never married because my mother hid it from her family. So, my mother kept her maiden name, and I had my father's name. It was always really awkward for me. Because of the feelings of illegitimacy, I made a vow to God that I would be married before I had children.

There were many times when I was a kid, I wished my father would come and take me away from my abusive situation with my mother. However, a little part of me was glad that I didn't get tossed back and forth every other weekend like my cousins did when they had visitation with their dad.

I saw firsthand how parents conspired and used their children to hurt each other. My cousins would turn into different people. As soon as things would start to normalize, it was time for them to go back with their dad. Sometimes they felt like they had to choose which parent they loved more. What a mess! Their parents used them as pawns because of their own mind games.

When my cousins' dad remarried, the woman he married had a daughter, and it seemed like he treated his stepdaughter better than he treated his own children. Eventually, he tried to get his child support reduced because he had a new family and couldn't be bothered with taking care of his children. My grandmother always told me, even though my cousins' parents were no longer married, at least they knew their dad.

My grandmother used to tell me she did extra things for me because my father was never around. Some of the extra things she would do for me ended up being a "bone of contention" and caused resentment toward me from my other cousins. At times, my grandmother was accused of playing favorites. When she became ill later, it turned out I was the only grandchild who would care for her.

After receiving the photos from my father, I would not contact him for another twenty-five years. I mailed him a card with a picture of my son from his college graduation. I addressed the envelope, and it sat on my desk for a month, as I prayed and debated if I should even mail it.

I did mail it, and a couple of weeks later I received a voicemail on my cell phone. When I returned home from work, I called my father back, and it was a very odd conversation. He acted like we were best buddies. All throughout the call, I hoped he would ask for forgiveness or admit what he had done was wrong, but he never did. My dad justified his actions by saying my grandfather was a bad person, and that my mom didn't want to have anything to do with him, so he left.

The topic of child support came up again, which touched a raw nerve in me, so I asked him why he kept bringing it up. In the back of my mind, I wondered about how my father handled conflict. It seemed as though when things got uncomfortable he just opted out and shut down. Ironically, I am the exact opposite.

I remember being very agitated on the phone when my father brought up the subject of child support again. He also said he wanted to have a relationship with me. I asked him, *"Why?"* I told him I knew my grandfather was a crazy man and that would explain part of the reason he stayed away. However, once I turned eighteen, he could have reached out to me. I told him he could have found me if he wanted to. I considered the fact that I had contacted him, as an adult, and gave him my address and phone number, which goes to show he took absolutely no initiative.

I proceeded to tell him my grandfather had been dead for twenty years and that his fear was no longer substantiated. I told him my grandmother had been dead for thirty years, and my mom had passed away in 1989. I also told him he was out of excuses.

My father then handed the phone to his wife, and we started to talk. The next part of the conversation left me speechless and frankly a little confused. His wife told me that when they moved to Oklahoma, shortly before they were born-again during the "Jesus Movement," both her and my father attended Rhema Bible College, in Oklahoma. After graduating, they moved to Las Vegas where apparently, my father planted a few churches.

I remember my mom telling me my dad never went anywhere without having a beer with him. This is truly an example of God's grace and forgiveness in my father's life. However, I do know he will still be held accountable for his lack of involvement in my life.

When I got off the phone, the Holy Spirit told me to get a notepad and pen and write down how much I thought my father owed me in back child support. So, I did. Then, the Holy Spirit told me to write down the times in my life when I received life-changing money. Now when I say life-changing, I mean a large amount of cash.

We received significant amounts of money from various sources. We received settlements from legal cases/disputes. Two years before my mom passed away, the Holy Spirit told me to buy a life insurance policy on her because she wouldn't live past fifty. She did not, and that was additional money coming our way.

When I totaled what I thought my father owed me, and the life-changing money which I had received up until that time, I heard the Holy Spirit say, *"See, things may not have been easy, but I always took care of you. You received more money than what your father owed in back child support. I AM your Father, and I always take care of the orphans and widows. I AM your source."*

I would later find out my father was only required to pay $33 a month in child support. I had estimated that he stopped paying child support when I was about eleven or twelve. He was required to pay $396.00 a year for the next seven years. This would have been $2772.00, if they had not required an increase. I received a lot more than $2772.00!

In 1996, I had a conversation with my husband, and I told him I had this weird feeling that I could somehow run into my father while we were living in California. My husband asked me if I would recognize him. I said, *"Oh yeah!"*

I later learned that my father, his wife, and my three siblings lived less than an hour away from me in Southern California, from 1996 to 2006. In 2006, they moved back to Oklahoma, which is the same year the LORD gave me the "Warwick Dream" and told me to go back to Detroit.

Since I had given my father my new address in California, he knew very well I was living there, although he may not have known the exact city. He could have found me if he wanted to.

I would later receive an email from my father's wife explaining more details of what led to them fleeing Michigan. She told me my grandfather Nick put a "contract" out on my father with the Greek mob from downtown Detroit. She said the same day that Aunt Star alerted them about what my grandfather had done, they were returning home and saw a stranger walking up the steps of their home. When he realized nobody was home, he eventually left. My father and his wife packed their belongings that night and left for Oklahoma.

She also said they struggled financially as a family—my father was in and out of work, and like us, they lived on welfare, and were always on the move. She said there was never a time that they didn't want to have anything to do with me, and that my dad was a prayer warrior, and had prayed for me every day of my life, since 1973. She said that my father not wanting to have anything to do with me was a lie from the pit of hell.

There was not a time during the correspondence of the emails or phone conversations that my father ever asked for forgiveness or attempted to apologize for his dereliction of duty as a father. In my opinion, he was only making excuses.

After I had time to process all this information, I heard the Holy Spirit clearly say I needed to forgive my father, and that all the years he was absent from my life, Abba (Father God in Hebrew) was my father.

Although my circumstances were less than perfect, and I had endured years of pain, misery, and abuse—Abba was always there. Abba was not happy with the abuse at the hands of my family, but I always knew that Abba loved me. I never recall blaming God for the things which happened to me. I just recall asking God to help me get through them, and He did.

Chapter 8

Government Housing and Life on Welfare

In Chapter 6, I mentioned my mom and I had to live in government housing. At the time, we were homeless and on a waiting list for an apartment. We ended up moving into the Colchester Apartments on Lotus Street, in Michigan, just west of Selfridge Air Force Base. For the most part, the apartment my mom and I resided in was fairly quiet. However, as you recall, my aunt Star and two cousins lived next door. There was constant foot traffic in and out of her apartment all day and night. In fact, there was so much foot traffic, she left her front door open most of the time.

I later discovered Aunt Star was the neighborhood drug dealer. Star sold everything from cocaine to pot, all types of various pills, and downers. The first time I had ever seen somebody on "speed" was her. I, inadvertently, walked into her bedroom to ask her a question and found her with a bong, needles, spoon, and candles. It wasn't until I became an adult that I remembered the incident and figured out what had been going on.

Every other weekend, my cousins would go with their dad, since Aunt Star and her husband divorced. One particular weekend when my cousins were gone, I remember walking in to the apartment building vestibule area, and one of the guys upstairs came running downstairs, yelling my aunt's name.

He walked by me as she exited her apartment, and he cocked a loaded gun to her head. I froze and thought, *"Oh my God, this guy is going to blow her brains out right in front of me!"*

Dottie was the lady who rented the apartment upstairs. She came rushing down the steps and tried to convince the gunman to put his gun down. By this time, I think someone had called the police. I tried to back out of the door, but he yelled at me and told me not to move. I was afraid he would shoot me. He and another man rented a room from Dottie. I believe they, too were drug dealers. I also think they were running a prostitution ring from upstairs. I'm not sure what happened that day to set this guy off, but I was sure glad when the police arrived. I later learned Aunt Star had cheated them out of some money.

My aunt Star constantly had people in her apartment using, buying, or selling drugs. Sometimes, Aunt Star would rent out her couch for some extra cash, so she could buy more drugs.

I wanted to be a good student and stay on the honor roll, so I always did my homework and tried to block out the chaos from Aunt Star's next door. Every once in a while, one of the drug addicts would knock on our door by mistake, looking for a fix. Thank God for peep holes!

I remember when I was younger, there would be times I could not go to sleep because of fear. I would listen to the radio all night. Sometimes, I would stay up all night because I wasn't sleepy. I also used to sleepwalk because there was so much stress in my life.

One night when I was sleep-walking, I ended up outside in the hallway under the stairs. I remember waking up because I was cold, and I had locked myself out of our apartment. I don't remember where my mom was. I had to beat on the door of my cousin's apartment and slept on their couch until the next day.

Aunt Star and my mom also used our free health insurance to their advantage. They used their Medicaid cards to visit various doctors to get prescription drugs to sell. (mom referred to the doctors she would get her drugs from as "Doctor Rocket.") My mother also worked as a bartender from time to time to bring in additional income.

Since my father did not pay child support and there was not enough money coming into the household—even with my mom's occasional bartending gigs, we were on welfare. Aunt Star got food stamps for three people, while my mom and I only got food stamps for the two of us. My mom would shop for hours and buy plain wrap everything. To this day, I cannot eat macaroni and cheese, fried bologna, or Ramen noodles. My mom always tried to make her food stamps stretch for the entire month.

Aunt Star, on the other hand, was not frugal with her food stamps. When Aunt Star ran out of food, she would complain to my mom. My mom would feel sorry for her and give her our food. Aunt Star was frivolous, wasteful, greedy, a cheat, and a liar. Not the best role model.

There were many months when we ran out of food. I would have to put water on my cereal and eat potato sandwiches. My mom would even shoplift, at times, because we ran out of money and food stamps. She had an extra-large purse and would steal lunchmeat and cheese, so we could eat.

There were many times we did not have enough food to eat, and I would go to bed hungry. We did use powdered milk when it was available, and sometimes got food baskets from the local Catholic charities.

A few times at Thanksgiving and Christmas, if it weren't for the church, we would not have had a holiday meal nor would we have received any Christmas gifts as kids.

Because we ran out of food so often, I tried taking matters into my own hands. There were some nice-looking pear, apple, and cherry trees just outside the apartment complex area. I went to go pick some fruit one day and started walking back to the apartment, carrying bags of fruit. I heard someone yell, *"Hey!"* When I turned around to look, there was a boy sitting on a branch in one of the trees. He threw a brick at my head.

I remember losing my balance and falling down. He got out of the tree and ran away. I remember picking myself up and staggering back to my apartment. My head felt like it swelled to twice its normal size, and I ended up with a concussion. No one was home at that time. I remember getting really sleepy. I went into my bedroom and sat on the bed in the corner of the wall to prop myself up. I was really scared because I could feel my head swelling. Everything was moving in slow motion, and I could see blood dripping down my face. It seemed like I sat there forever. Then I heard a voice say, *"Elizabeth don't go to sleep; stay awake and fight this. If you go to sleep, you might not wake up."*

I don't know who the voice belonged to. Was it an angel? Was it God? I remember staying up as long as I could, while looking at my alarm clock on the dresser. I stayed up for about two hours, crying out to God, and asking Him for help.

I couldn't fight it anymore. I had to go to sleep. It was about 4 o'clock in the afternoon. I slept the entire night and didn't wake up until the next morning. My mom called the police, and I gave them the description of the kid. I didn't recognize the kid from school or the apartment complex, and I never saw him again. This was one of the many traumatic things that happened to me as a child, but I believe God spared my life.

Although the stress I endured was enormous for any adult, let alone an eleven or twelve-year-old, I do have a few fond memories of my time in government housing. Halloween brings back good memories. The three of us and the kid next door, Mike, dressed up as the rock group KISS—a famous rock band from the 70's.

The following year at Halloween, it was 1977. *Star Wars* had just been released, but we couldn't afford costumes. So, we got creative and made paper-mache masks of Darth Vader, using black paint and Popsicle sticks. For the cape, we used an old, black bed sheet, and we dressed my cousin up as Darth Vader.

Earlier that year, my cousin Tim drove to Michigan from California in his VW bug. Tim had all of his belongings, along with a top-loading beta tape VCR, and his bootleg movies. A co-worker of mine asked me if I saw the original *Star Wars*. I told him, *"Yeah, like 362 times, thanks to cousin Tim!"*

As kids, we were always entrepreneurial because we never had any money. This time was no different. We charged the kids in the neighborhood $0.25 to come and watch, *Star Wars*. We also had lemonade stands, yard sales, and I babysat a lot. My biggest night to make money was New Year's Eve. Back then, for one kid I charged $25. One year a couple gave me $50.!

Keeping the money I made became a challenge. I had to hide it from my mom and Aunt Star or else they would take it from me. To prevent them from finding it, I converted my change into paper dollars and put the paper dollars in a sealed envelope. Then, I taped the sealed envelope on the backside of the picture frames hanging on my wall.

If I needed more space, I put the envelopes in between my mattress and box spring. I remember one year my grandmother gave me a $100 bill for my birthday. Grandmother said it wasn't much, but that she appreciated all the time I spent working for her at the bar, taking care of her and my grandfather.

Aunt Star's wild life and the abuse from my mother.

When she was able, my grandmother would buy me shoes and clothes if I needed them. One time I asked my grandmother for a pair of Nike shoes for the new school year. The shoes were $20, and that was a lot of money back then for one pair of shoes. She told me she would buy me the shoes, but they had to last all school year. Guess what? They did not last!

In fact, by the time Thanksgiving came around, the soles were beginning to separate from the shoes. However, they were the only pair of shoes I had. To preserve them, I used superglue, duct tape, and put cardboard inside the shoes. It was really cold that year. I decided the following year, I would go to Kmart and get a couple of pairs of shoes and a pair of boots for the $20 rather than another pair of Nike tennis shoes. Money was always tight. I received a lot of hand-me-downs, and we were regulars at local thrift stores.

The year my grandmother purchased the Nike shoes, she also bought me some clothes and a nice coat. After returning from a sleepover one night, I discovered Aunt Star raided my closet. Since we wore the same size clothes and shoes, she took my shoes, a jacket, and stained an outfit that I just got, and put it back in my closet- dirty. I immediately called my grandmother, who in turn called Aunt Star. The next thing I knew, Aunt Star was returning the rest of my belongings.

Aunt Star was a scammer, a thief, and a pathological liar. Her lies were so convincing and so elaborate, sometimes she actually believed her lies to be truth. After the incident with my clothing and shoes, she lied again. This time she stole a TV from my room and told my grandmother I said she could have it.

On another occasion years later, Aunt Star borrowed my grandmother's lawnmower and said my grandmother told her she could have it. We found out later, Aunt Star was running a "fencing ring" out of her basement. There were two guys in the neighborhood who would break into people's houses and garages to steal all types of equipment, tools, and bicycles. We learned that Aunt Star mistakenly sold my grandmother's lawnmower and didn't want anyone to know what she was doing.

When Aunt Star got caught in a lie, her voice would go up about five pitches, and she would start shouting you down, screaming, and cussing at you. I began to recognize her pattern. When she got caught in a lie, all "hell" would break loose!

My aunt Star was a "user." She used people and would discard them like trash, particularly men. She would try to get them to buy her things, pay her bills, and sell her drugs.

My mom's record wasn't clean, either. I learned that my mom was involved with this scumbag named, "Jack". He got my mom pregnant, and years later, I learned she had an abortion. I was saddened to learn this. This is one of the reasons I am pro-life. I named my brother, Josiah David and grieved my loss.

As I mentioned before, my mom was verbally and mentally abusive to me. One night, Aunt Star arranged a double-date for her and my mom. The men they were supposed to go on a date with seemed nice enough, but I said something to my mom she didn't like, and she started to beat me with a belt. The belt buckle had a little tooth of metal. When she started to hit me, she smacked my foot. My foot started to bleed, and I began to cry. I tried running away from my mom, but she grabbed me by the hair and started punching me in my face. I turned my face to avoid getting punching, and my face hit the corner of the wall. There was blood everywhere! I thought she had broken my nose. My face was bloodied and bruised for several weeks.

My earliest memory of punishment and beatings with the belt go back to when I was about four years old. My mom would grab whatever she could get her hands on; coat hangers, extension cords, and sometimes, she would beat me with a broom-stick handle. I would have welts and bruises on my body for weeks.

There was another occasion when I told my mom I wanted to live with my grandparents because I was tired of her giving our money and food stamps to Aunt Star. I told my mom I didn't care if my aunt and her kids didn't have enough food—that was their problem. My mom proceeded to have some type of volcanic episode and ran to the kitchen to grab a butcher knife. She held the knife to my throat and told me if I was ever disrespectful to her again, she would kill me. This eventually became a pattern. She didn't want to hit me. She just held a knife to my throat to scare and intimidate me.

Another time, I don't know if mom was on drugs or what was going on. It was a Saturday. My mom asked me a question, and obviously, she didn't like my answer. She ran to the kitchen and grabbed a butcher knife again. I started to run up the second flight of stairs, not thinking she would chase after me, but she did. She chased me up three flights of stairs and held the knife to my stomach.

She said again if I was ever disrespectful to her again, she would kill me. She told me I was nothing more than a "pain in the ass," and she wished I had never been born. At that moment, I wished I hadn't been born either!

The butcher knife became my mom's new weapon and method of punishment. If I said something she did not like, or if I gave her a dirty look, she would bolt to the kitchen and grab the butcher knife out of the drawer. The butcher knife had replaced the belt! Whenever I would see her dart off to the kitchen, I would run into my room and shut and lock the door behind me in hopes she would get tired and go away.

The next year I had a growth spurt, but my mom thought that I was still a punching bag. One day, she flipped out on me for no apparent reason. I raised my arms and hands over my head to protect my face, and she just kept beating on me. I kept asking her, *"What did I do; what did I do?"*

She didn't answer me, but a feeling of boldness rose up in me, and I pushed her down. She looked stunned, as I started to fight back. With shock on her face, I leaned over her, pointed to her, and told her if she ever hit me again, I was going to kill her. After that day, she never beat me again. I think I was about twelve or thirteen years old at the time.

Later, my mother told me that my grandmother wanted my mother to give me up for adoption. I think if abortion was legal when I was born, I probably would have been aborted, and this book would not have been written. My mother also told me she had taken some drugs in her first trimester to induce a miscarriage.

Chapter 9

Moving to California

At the beginning of this chapter I am going to provide a bit of context around the series of events which led to my family relocating from Michigan to California. I mentioned in Chapter 8, my cousin Tim drove from California to Michigan in the late 1970's to live. Later that year, my cousin Jack would follow. Jack and Tim were raised more like brothers than cousins. Tim's dad, Chris died suddenly from a heart attack in the 1960's, when Tim was a young boy. Jack's dad was my great-uncle Tony. Both Chris and Tony were my grandmother's brothers. Uncle Tony ended up raising my cousin Tim and his brother Gary as his own.

Jack had been born with a congenital eye defect and had many surgeries as a boy. I would later find out Jack would often be depressed, and he used lots of drugs. The worst place for Tim and Jack to stay was with my aunt Star, who as you now know, was the neighborhood drug dealer. Tim and Jack both dated and were romantically involved with somebody named Lynn. Aunt Star and Lynn were involved In a car accident that was caused by a drunk driver. Aunt Star was injured in the accident and required multiple surgeries, but they both survived the collision. Oddly enough, years later, Tim would be killed by a drunk driver.

Jack and Lynn eventually married and had a daughter. Lynn had a son from a prior marriage. Lynn eventually died from a heart attack, and Jack died of a brain aneurysm due to decades of drug use. Lynn's son from a prior marriage died in a car accident while he was driving drunk. Needless to say, there has been a lot of tragedy in my family. In one year alone, nine family members died.

Long before he passed away, my cousin Tim lived with my aunt Star for years, but eventually, we just lost touch with him. Years later, he contacted my grandparents, and we found out he was homeless, living at the rescue mission in downtown Detroit. My grandparents discussed allowing Tim to move in with us, but I had reservations —knowing his drug history and how he had issues keeping a job. My grandmother was very close with Tim's dad, Chris, and she felt obligated to take Tim in because he was her nephew

We arranged for transportation for Tim to come live with us, and he soon was hired at a bookstore in Ypsilanti, Michigan. Months later, Tim was doing so well, he was able to buy a car, another VW, for his commute to work. Tim was later promoted manager of the bookstore. One Saturday night, Tim needed to work late and was traveling home on the 275 expressway to Monroe. Unbeknownst to Tim, a lady driving a Pinto had entered the freeway going the wrong way, and collided with Tim's VW "head on."

About 3 A.M., we received a call from Uncle Tommy (my grandmother's other brother), saying that he received a call from a Michigan state trooper notifying him of Tim's accident. We later found out Tim did not have our phone number in his wallet.

    We ended up at a little hospital in Monroe, Michigan and entered the emergency room. As our eyes began to focus, we could see the figure of a man lying on a gurney on life support hooked up to I.V.'s. His body was severely bloated, and as we began to approach, it dawned on us this was my cousin Tim. He was almost unrecognizable.

    The entire event was so traumatizing to me, I had to run to the bathroom and throw water on my face. We all began to cry and were in shock that Tim was even able to survive the accident.

    Later, we found out that since the VW's trunk was in the front of the car, the roof of the car had imploded on Tim's head and crushed his skull. According to witnesses, the other driver was traveling at such a high rate of speed, that she pushed the front seat into the backseat. Tim's car was a mangled mess and looked like an accordion.

    Tim's injuries were so horrific, the small hospital in Monroe was not able to care for him. So, they airlifted him to a trauma center in Toledo, Ohio, which was approximately sixteen miles away.

    We reached out to all of the family and within twenty-four hours there were about fifty people at the hospital. Things were not looking any better for Tim. He was on life support, and everyone was in shock. The doctors conducted a brainwave on him. His EEG (an electroencephalogram (EEG) is a test that detects electrical activity in your brain), showed no brain activity. Because Tim was an organ donor, the hospital needed authorization from his mother, my aunt Mary, to disconnect him from the life support, and harvest his organs. During this time in the state of Ohio, an EEG test must have no brain activity for seventy-two hours before a "do not resuscitate order" is signed by the next of kin.

It was the longest three days of my life. I would later find out I had cousins who attended the same high school and didn't know they were related until their parents showed up at the hospital to visit Tim.

I remember the doctor talking to my aunt Mary and my cousin Gary, asking them if they'd made a decision on whether to pull the plug. They were still in shock and asked the whole family to gather for prayer in the conference room. Aunt Mary also wanted to find out how the rest of us felt about removing Tim from life support. If we waited too long to make a decision, some of Tim's organs would shut down and would be useless.

Aunt Mary decided to sign the "do not resuscitate order," and Tim was removed from life support. The family started to plan Tim's funeral and prepared to have his body sent back to California. It seemed like our entire life was in upheaval in less than a week.

We flew to Long Beach for Tim's funeral, and on the return flight, Aunt Kat and I discussed how our lives had changed. And, since my grandmother had passed away, and Tim had died such a violent death, we did not feel like there was anything keeping us in Michigan. We were ready for a change and had endured too many harsh winters in Michigan.

When we returned to Michigan, we had a serious conversation with my mom about moving to California. Aunt

Kat cashed in her retirement and arranged for a moving truck. By the end of March, we were in our cars and on our way to California.

I drove my Camaro with my mom as my passenger, along with my dog. My aunt Kat had my grandfather in her Trans Am, along with her cat. The entire drive from Michigan to California took us about a week. Since my grandfather was in a wheelchair and needed to stop each night, we were able to take our time.

On our way out West, my grandfather wanted to stop in Las Vegas and play blackjack. I had to sit at the table and show him the cards because the casino would not allow the cards to leave the table. My grandfather was in his wheelchair, so he was not able to sit at the blackjack table. Also, because of his stroke, he was very difficult to understand, but I learned to decipher what he was saying. We left the casino abruptly before we got kicked out, after he rudely accused the dealer of cheating!

My cousin's wife was the administrator of a nursing home, so once we arrived in California, she had a bed ready for my grandfather. That's where he stayed until he died.

Finding a job was not difficult. I arrived in California on Saturday and started working the following Monday with the help of employment agencies Aunt Kat and I had signed up for. In the meantime, my mom, Aunt Kat, and I slept in my cousin's fifth-wheel trailer in his driveway until we were able to find an apartment.

Making the transition from Michigan to California in some respects was easy but in some respects, was not. We entered an entire new culture where people had accents, and many folks were very rude. We had family members though, all over the place. Many of them frequently visited Michigan when we lived there but chose not to visit us because they didn't want to be around my grandfather when he was drunk, which was most of the time. Now that we were in California, they had a sudden desire for us to be part of their family. All these people felt like strangers to me.

There were many stories my grandmother told me about her brothers before she died. They claimed they wanted to be a family but were absent from our lives. My grandmother felt abandoned by her siblings. She suffered abuse in silence. Now, they wanted to be part of our lives? They gossiped about my grandparents when they were alive; now they wanted me to be part of their family. This all seemed to be a little hypocritical to me.

About a year later, I met my husband, and we were married. Ironically, for the first three years of our marriage, we lived in the house my uncle Chris and my aunt Mary purchased in the 1940's. Uncle Chris and Uncle Tony were honorably discharged from the military. Uncle Tony was in the Marines. Uncle Chris was in the Navy, and Uncle Tommy was in the Army. All had served during World War II.

My mom would later end up living with us in that rental home. She was my son's caregiver for the first year of his life. Sadly, because of her lifestyle of drug use and diabetes, her life was cut short.

Chapter 10

My Mother's Final Years

All throughout my life, I never remember my mom being healthy. She was diagnosed with diabetes when I was very young, and she was an insulin-dependent diabetic. Eventually, the diabetes would take my mom's eyesight and her life.

I later discovered all my mother's ailments and illnesses were attributed to her diet. Some doctor told her as a diabetic she could continue to eat bread and that fruit was considered "free." She interpreted this as meaning she could stuff as much fruit down her gullet as she wanted! This binge eating cycle of over-eating consumed her. She would eat until all the food in the house was gone. Over-eating made her blood sugar levels spike and required her to take even more insulin.

I have studied the effects of diabetes, as an adult, and my opinion is the doctor who told her she could still eat bread and fruit was a complete idiot! Her blood sugar was out of control almost daily. She ended up having to take two types of insulin through injections I gave her twice a day. Insulin, estrogen, and cortisol are fat-storing hormones. My mom's weight ballooned out of control.

She was on such massive amounts of insulin, it started to destroy her eyesight. She had laser surgery over a dozen times and eventually would go blind in one of her eyes. This would result in her losing her driving privileges. Eventually, without making corrections to her diet, the insulin would damage her kidneys, as well.

Mom would be on so much medication for her asthma, high blood pressure, and edema. With each new diagnosis, came a minimum of five more pills and medications that she was given. Not to mention all the side effects that came with the new pills. These pills, would in turn, have side effects which required even more medication. At some point, she was taking fifty+ pills a day.

I later found out her appendix was removed when she was five years old, which contributed to her having celiac disease. Celiac disease is the inability to digest grains and flour and can be life threatening. In the early 1980's, she would be diagnosed with osteoarthritis, slipped discs, and would have her gallbladder removed.

Because of the food allergies and out of control blood sugar, she would often have infections and cysts that would not heal because of the diabetes. My mom had several surgeries, and each time I was responsible for regularly changing her bandages and being her care giver.

Since my mom had terrible pain and problems with her eyesight, she used to tell everyone she had glaucoma. In her mind this was an excuse for her to smoke "pot." This was way before medical marijuana became a topic in the news.

When we lived in Michigan, she slipped on the ice and hurt her back. The back injury caused her to be immobile and eventually become addicted to pain medication. My mom used to be up all night eating and then would sleep all day. The more weight she gained, the more stress she put on her body. The more pain she was in, the less she moved. This started the vicious cycle all over again.

Toward the end, her kidneys started to shut down. The doctors would estimate she had over sixty pounds of excess water on her body (equal to about eight gallons of fluid). I remember one night I was getting ready to go to bed, and she looked at me with a spacey look in her eyes and dropped her bowl on the floor. I asked her what her name was and who the president was, and she could not answer me.

I got her dressed and immediately took her to the emergency room. Later, they contacted her doctor and implanted a shunt in her to start dialysis treatment.

My mom was often in and out of the hospital with congestive heart failure for most of my life. The fluid around her heart would cause her heart to have to pump harder. That, coupled with the extra weight, put an enormous amount of stress on her heart. She had half a dozen heart attacks and miraculously walked away from each one.

The doctors decided to put her on a ventilator in addition to the dialysis. She was on a ventilator a few years before, and the doctors told me there was a 50-50 chance she would come off of it. This time the doctors told me not to be very optimistic. During the first dialysis treatment, my mom went into cardiac arrest, and her heart stopped. They were able to resuscitate her, but she was on life support in the ICU for several days.

At that time in the state of California the next of kin had the option to sign a "do not resuscitate order" after seven days. Once my mom's EEG came back flat, I had to make a decision. I went home, talked with my aunt Kat, and my husband. We discussed what we would do.

The next day I went down to the hospital in Bellflower and signed the "do not resuscitate order." Shortly after that, they removed the ventilator from my mom, and she breathed on her own for about twelve hours. The next day, I received a call from the hospital that she had expired, and I needed to come down to sign the paperwork for her death certificate.

While I was filling out the paperwork for the death certificate, it seemed as if I were in a daze. I was by myself at the hospital, with no siblings, and at that moment it seemed like a relief. She had suffered so many years, and I suffered along with her because of her refusal to watch her diet and take care of herself. She would never see her grandson grow up.

Years later, I would hear the Holy Spirit say, *"Your great-grandmother died at eighty-nine, your grandmother died at sixty-five, and your mother died at forty-nine. Your mother cut her life in half because of her lifestyle and her stubbornness. It is My desire for My children to live long in the land."*

During this time, I was suffering with arthritis and some other physical ailments. I decided to contact a naturopathic doctor because I did not want my life to be cut short because of my choices. Even though I didn't smoke, drink, or do drugs, I wanted to be able to live long in the land and be an example to my family.

I would later do in-depth studies and take nursing classes to learn about diabetes and some of the ailments my mother had. I came to learn that the majority of her health conditions were preventable with a proper diet. It also appeared to me she didn't need any of the medications she was taking.

Today, I have a strong aversion to prescription medications. With the advent of the internet and the ability to learn about naturopathic medicine, I have discovered God has given us all kinds of natural remedies, so that our body can heal itself. However, we must get enough rest, avoid toxic water, grains, high fructose corn syrup, and all processed foods. I have come to the conclusion if man makes it, it's probably not good for you.

If I knew then what I know now, I would have taken my mother to another doctor who would teach her about nutrition. Then, I would have insisted she get counseling for the physical, verbal, and mental abuse she suffered as a child.

Chapter 11

How Stress and Trauma Enter

Trauma and abuse are typically a pattern. These behaviors are passed down from one generation to the next. Unless you know how to stop the pattern, you will continue to pass these behaviors on to your children and grandchildren. For me, it was finding out who Jesus was and how to apply the "blood" to the curses and sins in my life which were passed on through generations that were never dealt with in my family line, either spiritual or learned behavior.

Sin is something that goes all the way back to Adam and Eve in the Garden of Eden. In this section, I'm going to cover how I believe stress and trauma enter into a person's life through my own personal testimony, much of which you have read in the preceding chapters. This is not intended to diagnose or replace medical advice, counseling, or treatment that you are currently receiving or may need to receive. This is what I have learned through my many years of study, and these are things I have done to be completely delivered.

<u>**Deliverance**</u> **as stated in the Webster's dictionary:**

The act of speaking an opinion, decision, or verdict from a jury.

Deliver: *lead us not into temptation, to return stolen goods, to assist in giving birth, to send to an intended target or destination, to produce a promise.*

First, it is important to understand that most stress, trauma, and abuse are patterns. They are handed down from generation to generation, and unless you are born again, as a blood-bought believer in the Lord Jesus Christ, the cycle will likely continue to repeat itself. You have the authority to stop the transgressions (things you do to others) and iniquities (things that go on in your heart) from going to the third and fourth generation, and the power to ensure God's blessings go to the thousandth generation- See Isaiah 53.

In the Old Testament, we read God delivered His people, set them free from the bondage of earthly sin, and led them to a new life. For example, God delivered the children of Israel from their captivity in Egypt. He set a plan in motion for them to have new life and initiated a relationship with them which would bring healing to their souls.

In the New Testament when Jesus preached and taught, he laid hands on people, spoke the Word, and people were instantaneously delivered. See Mark 1:26 & Mark 5:13. (Please visit http://www.atfm.org Kingdom of God & Salvation)

Certain denominations look at what Jesus did in the Bible and teach that his working of miracles, signs, wonders, and casting out demons ceased with the apostles and the early church. However, since the enemy, Satan, was defeated at the cross, everything Jesus does in the New Testament, and what was written about in the Old Testament, still applies today. *"Jesus Christ is the same yesterday today and forever"* Hebrews 13:8.

Sadly, many churches today do not teach the Bible, and they contend the works of the ministry ended with the apostles. They incorrectly believe "deliverance" was only for that era but not for today.

This is why I believe we have so many immature Christians in the church still dealing with insecurity, inferiority, depression, and a whole host of other issues. It is because they are not searching the scripture for themselves to see their true identity in Jesus Christ and to see if His Word is true and apply it to their lives.

I have had conversations with pastors over the years, and they have expressed to me they believe in deliverance ministry, but it was not something they wanted to see in their church because it scared them. Sadly, this is the reason why I believe most Christians do not walk in victory and are still having issues. As believers, we must persevere and search the scriptures to find out the truth for ourselves.

The Bible teaches us that Christians can be demonically oppressed because we still have a flesh. At the point of salvation, our spirit man is instantly born again and has restored fellowship with the Father. However, since we still have a flesh, it takes a move of the Holy Spirit for us to realize we must put our flesh under subjection. We must also renew our mind and deal with the trauma and stress that has happened in our lives. We become a new creation in Christ, and therefore, we have to see ourselves as God sees us—complete in Christ.

Demonic spirits have the ability to put thoughts in our mind, to talk to us, torment, and harass us. In fact, as believers in the Lord Jesus Christ, we must learn how to exercise the power Jesus has given us. Demonic spirits, however, are not the source of every problem in a person's life. Some problems are just due to bad decisions, poor choices, and selfishness.

Jesus Christ has the ability to bring deliverance. Jesus Christ has authority over death, hell, the grave, and all demonic forces. Several years ago, I attempted to help people with deliverance, and the Lord told me something specific. He said, *"People don't want your help. They want you to do it for them."*

I spent years in church looking for help through prayer, attending Bible studies with church leadership, and found out no one could help me because they were not equipped. No one I sought out had ever suffered the level of abuse I had, and they just kept telling me to pray. Many of the Christians I encountered were immature, dealing with issues of insecurity and inferiority. The topic of deliverance just scared them!

One of the things I want you to understand is Jesus wants you to bear fruit—fruit that will remain! See John 15. Part of that fruit-bearing process is learning WHO the "vine dresser" is. Over the years, I have had conversations with pastors and others in church leadership about deliverance, and they just don't get it. And, they often mock things they don't understand. I believe many people are afraid of deliverance and possibly dealing with the sin in their life for fear of exposure.

Not everything a person is dealing with is attributed to demonic behavior that requires deliverance. A believer's mind MUST BE TRANSFORMED! People still have choices to make. The devil has a mission; he wants to kill, steal, and destroy the believer. If we are not strong in the Word, he can whisper thoughts to us, and we will think these thoughts are our own. Jesus said, *"My sheep hear My voice, and I know them, and they follow Me."* John 10:27. Obedience to God is the key to victory!

Often, people's issues will be revealed through subtle indicators and behaviors they have not been able to gain victory over. These issues may include (this list is not exhaustive): depression, anger, lust, pornography, fear, addictions, and abuse. Perhaps you or someone you know has tried repeatedly to just pray or read the Word, but this only results in temporary relief.

Some people may have tried medications, counseling behavior modification, and may seek deliverance ministry as a last resort. Successful deliverance bears good fruit that lasts. There is no need for a person to fear deliverance, and deliverance does not need to be sensationalized. When some people think of deliverance, they have images of people yelling and screaming, and they imagine an atmosphere of confusion. You don't need to yell, scream, or have it look like a circus for deliverance to take place.

The apostle Paul tells us the fruit of the Holy Spirit in Galatians 5:22, includes: *love, joy, peace, patience, kindness, and self-control*. It is vital you study God's Word if you are truly seeking deliverance in your life. **It is not considered a weakness to ask the Holy Spirit for help!**

There is no magic bullet, no quick fix, and no magic wand to being delivered. It may happen over time, or the Holy Spirit can heal some things in an instant.

Another way stress and trauma can enter your life is by physical accidents. This could be physical, mental, or verbal abuse. It can be car accidents! Maybe when you were a kid, you swore a blood oath, played with the Ouija board, or went to a séance at somebody's house. And, unbeknownst to you, you got involved with the occult, fortune-telling, tarot cards, or perhaps you have watched occult movies. All these issues need to be addressed.

Many years ago, I felt my Christian walk was dry and stagnant. I wanted to go further with the Lord. There were many folks in my church who were just going through the motions and were not living a victorious life. Many of them had been saved for decades and were still dealing with addictions, anger, relationship problems, money problems, and all kinds of garbage. I didn't want that life.

I had a serious conversation with the Lord, and I wrote down some of the things He told me. What He told me may not be the exact thing He's going to tell you. This is just a blueprint and a guideline. Ask God what you need to do. Your past is part of you, but don't let it dictate your future.

Chapter 12

Ten Steps to be Set Free

Step 1: Confess you are a sinner! Repent-Repent–Repent

The word **"repent"** means you have to turn around and go the opposite direction. I'm just going to be blunt and come out and say it—if you're still dealing with the same stuff that you've been dealing with for years, don't expect anything to change until you change what you're doing! If you keep doing things your way, you will continue to get the same results.

By now you should be able to see your way doesn't work! Only God's way works. It's time to stop playing around. It's time to stop playing church and going through the motions. Church is not the kingdom! God has a standard, and if your way worked, you'd be delivered already—**boom!**
Do you really want help for yourself? If you seek outside ministerial resources, ask yourself the following questions:

Are you willing to do the homework?

Are you willing to show up for the sessions?

Are you willing to face the truth about yourself?

Are you willing to listen to the voice of the Holy Spirit, move forward, and do what He tells you to do?

Are you willing to give up your sin?

The first order of business is to be saved. Are you born again? There are people sitting in churches all across the world who believe they're saved, but what if they aren't?

Step 2: Pray this prayer daily until you feel things break off of you!

My Deliverance Prayer

Heavenly Father, I come to you now in Jesus' name to repent of all the sins in my life and also in the lives of my ancestors that may have resulted in a curse. I repent of all disobedience, rebellion, mistreatment of others, lying, cheating, and using or slandering Your name in vain. I repent of all perversion, lust, incest, fornication, adultery, idolatry, witchcraft, murder, and any occult involvement.

Heavenly Father, I ask for Your forgiveness and cleansing through the blood of Your Son—The Lord Jesus Christ. Lord Jesus, I now take the authority You have given me and ask that You anoint me now as I command all demonic spirits of anger, rage, fear, depression, destruction, torment, guilt, bondage, vagabond, lying, manipulation, twisting words of deception, distortion, rejection, unforgiveness, bitterness, mind-control, double-mindedness, confusion, passivity, sickness, disease, pain, food addictions, alcohol, drugs, sexual sin, fornication, adultery, molestation, laziness, procrastination, pornography, gambling, whoredom, python, Ahab, Jezebel, chaos, tornado spirits, the spirit of the Jester, and nicotine to come out in the name of Jesus. No demonic spirit is welcome in this holy temple!

I break all spoken curses and spells that may have been performed over my life and any curses resulting from involvement with Ouija boards, psychics, tarot cards, horoscopes, secular music or through T ,V, movies and pornography.

I break all curses off my family, marriage, children, and relatives. I break every shackle, chain, cord, habit, craving, debt, soul-ties, and spirits that have tried to rob, kill, or destroy my life. I command my family to be set free! I break every demonic assignment over my family. Satan, loose them now! In Jesus' name! According to Galatians 3:13, Christ has redeemed us from the curse of the law.

Jesus Christ is the way, the truth, and the life. I am now God's child, and through my Lord Jesus I am able to cast down all demonic powers and spirits that come against me or my family. I am not cursed but blessed! I am blessed coming in and blessed going out. I am above and not beneath. I am the head and not the tail. I am blessed, and what God has blessed cannot be cursed.

I am free, and I am saved. I have now exercised my faith and know that this confession is made unto salvation according to Romans 10:9-10. All my sins have been remitted, and I am loosed from the curse that came as a result of disobedience and rebellion to the Word of God. Thank You, Heavenly Father; thank You, Lord Jesus; thank You, Holy Spirit for forgiving me and loving me.

Thank You for setting me free from every curse and spirit that has operated in my life. Father God, I pray for discernment and for a new vision to help me recognize and *resist all evil and all fleshly, worldly ways. I am anointed through the Lord, Jesus Christ. I thank You, Jesus for Your guidance and discipline as I continue to be a victorious soldier and holy child. AMEN!*

You must decide to rid yourself of sin and demonic influences.

ANYTHING OR ANYONE YOU CANNOT GIVE UP IS AN IDOL IN YOUR LIFE!

CHOOSE this day whom you will serve!

Step 3: Assume the position through prayer!

Do you want to hear God's voice?

Then it's time to shut up!

Get on the floor, turn on some worship music, and don't get up until God changes you.

I'm not going to put a heavy load on you and tell you that you MUST pray sixteen hours a day to get delivered. Don't make prayer a law! It is not reflected that way in Scripture. I see Jesus telling evil spirits to get out, and they leave. However, if you don't tell the evil spirits to get out, they are not going to leave. I have prayed over people, and the Lord has revealed to me supernatural and demonic influences in their lives that they don't want to get rid of.

I was praying over a young woman, and the Lord showed me she had a spirit of depression which was a "familiar spirit" that she carried around with her like a blanket. The woman told me the blanket of depression had been with her as far back as she could remember, and she was comfortable with it.

As I ministered to this woman further, I found out her mother had been a prostitute, that she was conceived in a brothel, and her mother was involved in occult activities. This poor, young woman did not even know who her father was, but Jesus wanted to be her Father that day!

Although this young woman was married, she was involved in multiple, adulterous affairs and had been promiscuous from a very young age. Her perception of herself was she was not worth saving, and she did not deserve better.

Please get a revelation of this! The enemy wants to distort everything God has made you to be. You really do have the ability to renew your mind and to tell the demonic forces to leave. Every person God has created has worth and value, and when we fail to see that, we allow the enemy to wreak havoc in our lives. **If you don't tell the evil spirits to get out, they are going to be there until you tell them to leave.**

Here is a variation of a prayer I have used in my own life:

Heavenly Father, I thank You that You are God. You love me, and You answer prayer. As a blood-bought believer in the Lord, Jesus Christ, I take authority over all demonic influences over my body, my mind, my family, my job, and all of my property, which goes back to Adam and Eve. I ask You, Father, to cut off all hindrances, obstacles, blockages, and delays to my deliverance and healing. I serve a written order of divorcement, a written order of eviction to the enemy and everything that is attached to him—to the root of the demonic influences, and I command them to go by the power and blood of Jesus Christ, the Messiah, Who has been given all power and authority by the Father, God to set me free. I ask You to close ungodly open doors that give the enemy access in my life. By faith, I acknowledge You are my Lord and my Savior. You died for me, so I will live for You. Please restore everything the enemy has stolen because the enemy is under my feet.

Step 4: Read the Bible

Once you have made the decision you are going to do whatever it takes to be free, you have to read your Bible and memorize scripture! You can no longer rely on the pastor, minister, or priest to tell you what the Word says. You have to memorize it and know it YOURSELF! It's the truth about yourself that will set you free.

    I have noticed a disturbing trend over the years. People do not take their Bibles to church anymore! This needs to change, and it needs to start with us. Learn how to study your Bible. Take an inductive Bible study course. Get a good college dictionary and find a Bible program. There are many resources online—some are FREE! You can listen to the Bible in audio form. You can buy videos and watch them. You can do all the above. You must be willing to do whatever it takes to be delivered!

    If you are a blood-bought believer in the Lord, Jesus Christ, you are now in relationship with the Savior. It is now time for you to study the Word and find out who He is! Do you go to church, yet have a hypocritical and superficial relationship with the Lord? You can change that right now.

Step 5: Forgiveness

If you do not learn to forgive, you will stagnate in your walk. Look, please do not take my words as some type of free "pass" for everyone who has mistreated you. That's not what I'm saying. When you hold unforgiveness in your heart, it is like you are drinking poison and expecting the other person to die. I am convinced unforgiveness is the primary blockage that grieves the Holy Spirit and prevents change in people's lives. Unforgiveness keeps people in bondage mentally and physically.

Step 6: The fear of the Lord

Proverbs says the fear of the Lord is the beginning of wisdom. I'm not talking about being afraid of the Lord but having a healthy reverence and respect for the God of the universe. He's not your pal. He's not your buddy, and He's certainly not your homeboy! He is God Almighty, Creator of the universe! Get a revelation of this!

Step 7: Get in God's presence

Once you have admitted you have a problem, you need God's help. Now that you have a healthy reverence and respect for Who He is, get in His presence. The Creator of the universe loves you. He wants what's best for you. The Lord God Almighty is always kind, always gracious, always righteous, always merciful, always loving, and HE wants to spend time with you. Anything opposite to these characteristics comes from the enemy. Read First Corinthians 13.

Step 8: Cut out distractions

Remove chaos, cut off toxic relationships, stop being co-dependent, stop thinking you have to fix everybody, and stop talking to everyone about all of your problems! Go talk to Jesus!

Step 9: Don't run to the phone; run to the THRONE!

Jesus wants to be your source! Turn off the television, computer, get off the phone, and stop being distracted by inconsequential drivel that will have no eternal value. If you are too busy to study and spend time with God, YOU ARE TOO BUSY!

Step 10: Take care of yourself

If you are dealing with health issues and conditions, you may have demonic strongholds in your life. Health conditions like the ones my mother suffered from are often self-inflicted. Are you eating properly, getting enough sleep, drinking enough water, and getting an appropriate amount of exercise? You will not be able to fulfill the calling on your life if you are sick and have strongholds in your life.

<u>The deliverance process as I see it</u>

A caring and loving Christian can help you with all ten of these steps. Some of them will be easier than others. You can meet with the leadership in your church and have someone coach you to come up with a plan and accountability to help you through your journey.

I didn't have anybody in my church who was capable or knowledgeable about these issues to help me. It was literally me and the Holy Spirit. All this information I am sharing were things I did in my own life. I have spent significant amounts of time and money on this—reading, praying, watching videos, going to seminars, obtaining degrees, and sifting through information online. This process takes time. I have condensed decades of information in this book. Your issues will be very specific to you, so please remember this is just an outline.

One of the things I figured out was when the Holy Spirit told me to do one thing, and I did it, that's when the Holy Spirit told me to do the next thing. There was a specific progression of things I needed to do in my life, and I had to deal with them one at a time, as to not be overwhelmed by it all.

Exercise

I remember reading a book by Marilyn Hickey called, *Next-Generation Blessings*. In the book, Marilyn Hickey recommends you make a list of all the sins you're dealing with, and go back and make a list of all the sins in your family line that you know of. I want you to do this now. Think about your own sins and the sins of your family members—your grandparents, great-grandparents, parents, uncles, siblings, etc. Write the sins on a piece of paper, pray over them, ask

Jesus to cut everything off, and cover them in the blood. After you've done that, **burn the paper.**

Chapter 13

Living Victoriously

We must walk in forgiveness.

We are taught as Christians that when we went down to the altar and asked Jesus into our heart, all our sins were forgiven, and they are. However, our soul is still being restored, and the Holy Spirit may deal with us one issue at a time.

I remember an instance when I was sitting in my house talking to the Lord. I asked Him a question, *"Lord, I have been a believer for a few years now. I feel like I've hit a wall, and there's blockage. Would you please show me what it is?"*

Guess what? The Lord did show me what it was. Never ask the Lord a question you don't really want to know the answer to. He told me I was harboring unforgiveness in my heart, and that if I didn't forgive certain people, I could not go any farther with Him. Well, let's just say I got a little irritated when I heard that. I said, *"God, You know what they did to me! Is this even possible that I could forgive them? They don't deserve my forgiveness!"*

Then I heard the Lord say, *"If I could forgive you, you can forgive others. I would never tell you something that wasn't in My Word or something you could not do."*

I made a list of names. I went down the list, and I said, **"Lord, as an act of my will I choose to forgive because you forgave me, and you said if I didn't forgive others, you could not forgive me."**

When I started to make the list, I put down the person's offense(s) that were committed against me next to their name. I kept praying every day until I felt a breakthrough and release over each person. One thing you can use to measure if you really have forgiven someone, is when you hear their name mentioned in a conversation or see them out somewhere, you don't get that sinking feeling in the pit of your stomach. You no longer have that urge to go up and slap them!

The Lord also told me something very interesting. He said just because I had forgiven them didn't mean I had to be in relationship with them. Nor did it mean what they did to me was okay. He told me as long as I held unforgiveness against these people, I was the one who was instituting judgment and punishment not Him.

Meeting with a pastor, Christian counselor, or mature friend can help you pinpoint certain areas and issues in your life. This is an important step in finding your identity in Christ. Once the Lord started to reveal to me about strongholds, demonic thought processes, and the sins in my family, I sought out self-deliverance teachings.

Sometimes, the Lord would just give me one word like "Jezebel", "Spirit of the Jester", or "Ahab", and I would need to search these things out. It was like a scavenger hunt. As I studied, I realized it was God's mercy that He was showing me these things.

Remember, when you became a Christian, you took the Lord's name that day. It is similar to being married. On your wedding day, if you are the bride, you took the groom's name that day.

I started attending "healing" rooms. A healing room is a place where the attending believers should be very mature and well-versed in identifying, seeing, hearing, or feeling strongholds in a person's life that need to be addressed. I went to several healing rooms and would feel temporary relief but wasn't quite sure what the main issue was, until I went to this one specific healing room. I filled out the short application about stuff that happened in my life, sat down in a chair, and an older couple began to pray for me. The older gentleman didn't want to see my paper. He just started praying what the Holy Spirit showed him. When he was done, I felt a huge release. He did something specific. He prayed the "Father's blessing" over me that Abraham did in the Old Testament. He stood in as a surrogate father because my father was not around. It was at that point I felt all kinds of critters break off of me.

I visited the healing room a few more times and several years later, I ran into the older couple at a healing revival! God is good!

Your identity is not what is done to you. Your identity is in the ONE Who died for you.

How we see ourselves and how we think about ourselves, changes our perception and our moods. The Bible says *as a man thinks about himself in his heart, so is he.* Proverbs 23:7. If we believe we are damaged or have been told we are useless, dirty, or have been violated in a sexual way, that's how we see ourselves—as a victim.

Self-pity

I have prayed for numerous people over the years, and victims of abuse often feel sorry for themselves. Self-pity is idolatry. Idolatry is putting yourself on the throne rather than God being on the throne. God wants us to be a living sacrifice. Well, guess what? Living sacrifices crawl off the altar. Self-pity is attached to depression, bipolar disorder, suicidal thoughts, alcoholism, and drug addiction.

Experiencing Deliverance Ministry

It seemed like my entire life I always attracted the neediest, most high- maintenance people who could not do anything for themselves. Many of them thought the purpose of my life was to make their life easier. I do not think I gave off that impression, but sometimes when I was busy or unable to help someone—their beast was unleashed. If it was in business or at church, they just became angry, slanderous, and would start to insult me with name-calling, cussing at me, and trying to bully me. I remember this happening to me as a child. However, most people who endure this type of bullying and manipulation turn into "people pleasers." This means they cannot take the rejection or the thought of losing a friendship, particularly if they are co-dependent.

There were many people who thought my entire life was wrapped up in doing their bidding and serving them. As I started to cut off toxic relationships–whether they were friends, pastors and church leaders, co-workers, or family members, a pattern started to emerge in all of these relationships. They all wanted to control me! When I would speak up for myself—which was often—and they figured out they couldn't control me, a confrontation would ensue.

This basically meant if I would not let them control me, they were going to end the relationship. They would tell me I was in rebellion to them. Many of these folks are no longer in ministry. The lesson here is to know that God will handle His business when His children are being abused in His name.

I noticed when I needed something or if I had an emergency, these people were always too busy to pick up the phone. Some people just stopped calling me altogether which worked out for my good.

It was at that point the Lord told me I needed to take everything a step further and seek out the help of a deliverance ministry. I made an appointment with a ministry in Hesperia, CA. I met with a woman named Melissa for a three-hour session. She told me when she first met me, she saw in the "spirit", a helmet on my head, with several cable and antennae on and around me like a satellite.

She said she believed it was something generational, and it was pulling in all of these generational curses and spirits that wanted to control me. One of the issues which came up in the deliverance ministry session was my grandfather's alcoholism and his involvement with "Freemasonry". The Freemasons are a cult that gave birth to Mormonism. Mormonism gave birth to Jehovah's Witnesses. All of these organizations deny the deity of Christ and are satanic in nature and occult in practice.

After my session, the Lord revealed a whole bunch of stuff. A pastor told us, (I was on their staff at this time as the associate and youth pastor) they wanted my gifts, but they didn't want me. They wanted to control our lives, our schedule, how I raised my son, commented on where I went on vacation, made comments as to how I spent my money, and who my friends were.

At one point, the pastor's wife attempted to control how I wore my hair and what color clothing I wore to church. This is the "Jezebel" spirit of intimidation and control. You must learn to deal with it if you have this in your life. When the pastors figured out they couldn't manipulate me, they started to call my friends and church members and started to gossip about me. Yes, these were the pastors who are no longer pastors because this was their standard and how horribly they treated people.

My personal reflections

I have been in ministry a very long time and prior to that my grandparents owned a bar. I was around drug addicts, alcoholics, bikers, prostitutes, thieves, and God knows what else. I asked the Lord, Who knows the answer to every unanswered question, *"Why do some people drink alcohol and take downers, and why do other people get hooked on speed and caffeine?"* The Lord told me something very interesting. He said people who use pot, alcohol, downers, and shoot heroin are opting out of life. Something happened to them so traumatic that they just always want to be high, so they don't have to think about or deal with their issues and trauma.

On the flipside, people who use cocaine, speed or caffeine, don't like themselves. They can't sit still long enough because they do not like who they are, and their life is in chaos. If they sit still too long, they have to deal with their problems, and they can't because they don't know how. **This is why they need Jesus.**

Many abused people make it their goal in life to control every circumstance, every conversation, and every aspect of every area of life in the people they associate with. These are the people who comment on everything, from your hairstyle, your clothing, your shoes, to what kind of car you drive, what kind of food you eat, how you spend your money, where you go on vacation, the books you read, what you watch on TV, etc. You can never do anything right according to them.

Everything you do is wrong in their eyes and is a personal affront to them. If the controlling person is offended, he or she takes everything personally. They want you to get their permission for everything. They feel it is their goal in life to run your life. This is how you can tell a damaged person. **Subconsciously, they want to control every situation, so they will never be hurt again.**

When you do hurt them, inadvertently, or a perceived violation occurs in some way, they will abruptly cut you off and never tell you what happened. This is because they hate confrontation and will blame you for every bad thing that happens to them. **Some of these folks have passive-aggressive personalities.**

These are the people who manipulate with anger, fear, violence, and intimidation. This includes women who can fake crocodile tears and cry at the drop of a hat to manipulate men into doing what they want. If they can't control you, they will threaten to pull you out of ministry. The master manipulator will use rejection, money, and sex to gain control of his or her victims.

Remember, the main point is to control people's lives. If you are curious about how to identify some of these demonic spirits, specifically "Jezebel," when it tries to control you, tell it, "NO!" Watch the response you get. Either this person will fly off into a volcanic rage or will start crying to manipulate you.

Have you ever been sitting in a room when someone walks in, and you can just feel the chaos on them? They whip everybody up into a tornado? A tornado only leaves devastation and destruction in its path. Do you know somebody like this? People start to get agitated, start strife, and distortion; people get sarcastic and nasty. Well, this is the spirit of chaos!

Also, when people have used large amounts of drugs, it damages the brain. That's why people who have used crack cocaine can't sit still for more than five seconds. They always have to be walking around because they have "jacked up" the neurons in their brain. They have a hard time remembering things, so it appears that they lie all the time, but the fact is sometimes they just can't remember what they told anybody.

Jesus restores all things!

It's time to renounce witchcraft and rebellion. If you have opened the door to self-medicating, you must confess it and move on. If you really seek deliverance in your life and truly want to be healed in areas—**you must do whatever it takes to get healed!**

If I told you, you had a disease, you would probably want to go to the best doctors at the best hospitals, and receive the best treatment. Sin is a disease that kills everyone! Jesus is the best doctor. The best hospital is a good church. The best treatment is to let the Holy Spirit in to restore your soul. Your soul is your mind, your will, and your emotions.

Final Exercise

If you've never received Jesus Christ as your Lord and Savior, you should do that now. No amount of counseling, meditation, or behavioral therapy is going to change your situation if you do not know Jesus as your personal Lord and Savior.

Finally, read Psalm 23, and put your name in the place of the personal pronouns.

A prayer by faith to be "Born Again"

Dear Lord Jesus:

I acknowledge I have broken Your laws, sinned against You, and I need a Savior. I believe and confess with my mouth that You are the only God, and Jesus died on the cross to pay for my sins because I can't pay for them myself. Hell is a real place. Jesus died for me, so I do not have to go to hell. Jesus, I give You permission by Your Holy Spirit to come live in my heart, and I surrender my life to You. Please apply Your perfect, sinless blood to my sin debt. I repent (I turn away from all sin) and renounce (to give up by formal announcement to relinquish, to reject, disown, stop practicing) my old, ungodly ways. Help me to learn, understand, remember, and live by Your Word. Fill me with Your Holy Spirit. Help me to follow You all the days of my life. I ask You, LORD to baptize me with Your Holy Spirit and fill me with Your love, so I can walk in fullness!

I am now "born again" by faith in Your Holy Spirit, and I receive Your forgiveness. I ask that You baptize me in Your love and give me wisdom and revelation in the knowledge of You. Help me to live out Your divine plan in my life. Show me the things I need to change and heal my pain from those who have hurt and wounded me. Help me to forgive others as You have forgiven me. Use me to fulfill Your purpose and plan. I also believe that one day Jesus will return to earth, and God will set up His kingdom.

The battle belongs to the Lord! Come forth! It's time to take off your grave clothes!

ABOUT THE AUTHOR

Dr. E.M. Ernst *is an anointed teacher with a unique and powerful gift for imparting the Word of God.*

Her anointed messages are filled with common sense, humor, and a heart to instill God's Word in believers with authority, clarity, and personal application.

Dr. Ernst *believes that the LORD wants to impart His gifts to all believers! Her desire is to bridge the gap between the generations with Yeshua as the Center of the church! The "Kingdom of God" is NOT a religion; it is the King's Domain.*

Dr. Ernst's *teaching helps people understand a clearer path into transformation. Her unique style and humor is taken from real-life experiences that keep you smiling, as the truth hits home.*

Since coming to Christ, Dr. Ernst has served in ministry in various levels of leadership, such as Children's, Youth, and as Associate/Administrative Pastor.

Over the years, Dr. Ernst and her husband have ministered to local youth, college and career groups, have been camp counselors, and led local outreaches. She currently resides in Southern California and has expanded the ministry outreach in media to reach the "Josiah Generation."

www.atfm.org©

Against the Flow T.V. Show ©

Josiah Generation Arts & Media **YouTube Channel**©

https://www.facebook.com/JosiahGenerationArtsandMedia/©

www.ingramcontent.com/pod-product-compliance
Lightning Source LLC
Chambersburg PA
CBHW031401040426
42444CB00005B/381